Survival Manual

to
Divorce

Survival Manual
to
Divorce

Your Guide to Financial Confidence & Prosperity

Carol Ann Wilson

MARKETPLACE BOOKS, INC.
Columbia, Maryland

ISBN 1-59280-193-5

Printed in the United States of America.

1 2 3 4 5 6 7 8 9 0

To my husband, Bill Fullmer, who showed me that there is life after divorce.

"Divorce is often the biggest psychological crisis of an individual's life: that is, unless a child or spouse has died. On the stress 'Richter Scale' divorce is in the top three."

— Dr. Judith Briles
Author of *The Dollars and Sense of Divorce*

contents

acknowledgements

To Judith Briles, a friend and mentor, to whom I am so indebted that I can never repay all of the help she has given to me;

To Alan Gappinger, who has always been there to answer questions, provide clarification, and insight;

To Barbara Stark, Helen Stone, Ed Schilling, Christine Coates, Michael Caplan, and Gail Heinzman for their contributions;

And to my husband, Bill Fullmer, whose understanding and support has been truly instrumental in the writing of this book.

introduction

In the early 1980's I was hired by a woman from Connecticut who was getting divorced. She wanted me to represent her in court as an expert witness. Armed with my charts and graphs, I was ready to show why she should in fact get the property and alimony award she was requesting.

It was during this proceeding that the notion of using my financial planning background to aid in equitable divorce settlements came to me. In meeting with several individuals after their divorces were final, they seemed to be in severe financial trouble — a trend that continued to increase the more research I did. Yet, I could not understand how they were winding up in such poverty when their martial assets had been divided evenly — they shouldn't be having these financial problems. It was from these encounters and my ensuing research that lead me to develop a software program called "DivorceCalc™" that clearly showed, in black and white, that *equal is not always equitable!*

Based upon the questions I've been asked over the years, I saw that there was a need for a simple, straightforward book on divorce and the financial repercussions to an inequitable settlement. There are books on the market that go into great detail about the emotional, financial, and legal aspects of divorce. But many times all that is needed is a brief explanation, in plain English, of the basics of the divorce process.

I believe this is that book.

WHO needs this book?
- Anyone going through a divorce or separation.

WHAT can it do for me?
- Give you a general understanding of the divorce process.

WHAT will it *not* do for me?
- Give you all you need to know to represent yourself. By necessity, some answers are in general terms because the law varies from state-to-state. Always depend on your lawyer for legal advice.

WHEN do I need to read it?

- As soon as you see there is a problem in your marriage.

WHY was this book written?

- Because there was a need for a concise explanation of the divorce process in everyday language.

I wish that there wasn't a need for this type of book. But divorce is a reality. Sometimes, despite the best efforts of good people, marriages break up. When that happens you need sound advise both financial and legal. While this book won't provide the information needed to represent yourself in a court of law, it will provide you with a strong foundation of knowledge that will empower you to make informed decisions and work you through the process as painlessly as possible. Best of luck to you as you go through this process.

Carol Ann Wilson
January 2005

PART 1

THE PREPARATION PROCESS

THE REALITY OF DIVORCE: NOT JUST SOMETHING THAT HAPPENS TO "OTHER PEOPLE" ANYMORE

Most people enter marriage believing in the words "till death do us part." They vow that *their* marriage will last forever. They won't make those mistakes that "other people" make. They will beat the divorce odds. And for a while they do. Then something happens and before they realize it, they have indeed become just another one of the divorce statistics.

Divorce isn't something that just happens to "other people" anymore. In fact, according to the last collection of detailed information on marriage and divorce by the National Center for Health Statistics (NCHS) gathered in 1996, there are about 1.2 million divorces every year in the United States. That's at least 2.4 million people who must face the devastation of a break-up and the ensuing challenges that will undoubtedly follow.

> **The solution is often not to prevent the divorce but to help move the process along as painlessly as possible.**

As the U.S. Department of Health and Human Services, Centers for Disease Control and Prevention, and the National Center for Health Statistics have concluded in their statistical analysis: In 1997, there were 2,384,000 marriages and 1,163,000 divorces which meant there were 49% as many divorces as marriages. In 1998, there were 2,244,000 marriages and 1,135,000 divorces which meant there were 51% as many divorces as marriages.

> ## It is an unfortunate truth that divorce is a fact of life in the United States.

This does not mean that 51% of *all* marriages will fail. These numbers simply represent the cold hard fact that divorce can and does happen. However, the solution is often not to prevent divorce but to help move the process along as painlessly as possible. While there are some couples who are able to remain cordial throughout effecting a somewhat civilized divorce, more often then not, most couples experience World War III. Heightened emotional state of minds coupled with the stress of the judicial process can lead to damaging outcomes lasting a lifetime. Yet, can we think that there may be a way to lesson the negative impact on all involved? Are equitable settlements really a possibility?

Contrary to popular belief, arranging an equitable settlement is not only achievable but can be done in such a manner that even though a reduced standard of living may be forseen, it doesn't have to be the dramatic decrease each spouse anticipates. This has created a real market niche for professionals who are needed in all phases of the divorce process.

Educated divorce specialists and sophisticated software methodology such as The DivorceCalc™ can be used to accomplish a more humane outcome. But first let's take a look at the issues facing each spouse. Enter the Financial Divorce Specialist.

HER SIDE: FINANCIAL SURVIVAL

Despite the women's movement and the continued strides for equality being made in the workforce, today's family is more "traditional" then society would give credit for. The higher the income of the family, the wider the financial gap between divorced partners. The reason? Even though society is changing, most couples still invest in the husband's career (Breadwinner Dad) while the wife's job (Homemaker Mom) takes second place. And if the marriage has lasted a long time, the wife has potentially lost at least a decade of career growth if not more. Although a number of recent changes have started to alter this pattern, making it more "atypical" then "typical," most divorcing couples began their marriages in this traditional format.

> **Even though society is changing, most couples still invest in the husband's career (Breadwinner Dad) while the wife's job (Homemaker Mom) takes second place.**

The bottom line: Divorcing men and women simply do not have equal income-producing potential. Instead, women who have spent 20 or 30 years in traditional marriages find themselves out in the cold with minimal marketable skills and minimal real job prospects.

The courts often ignore this crucial issue when dividing marital property. Most lawyers and judges try to provide equitable divorce settlements for both parties. However, without a comprehensive financial analysis, many wives end up in dire financial straits despite legislation designed to provide fair divorce settlements. A number of factors can contribute to an imbalance in a divorce settlement; however, one fundamental fact prevails: *a traditional married couple's lifestyle is usually based on the husband's income.*

In dividing marital property, courts traditionally have overlooked one major asset of a marriage: the husband's career and the assets associated with it. These can include his:

- Salary
- Stock options
- Health insurance
- Life insurance
- Disability insurance
- Vacation pay
- Sick pay
- Education and training
- Seniority and networking
- Potential earning power

Unfortunately, many courts don't recognize career assets as property. In creating an equitable financial settlement, it is important to remember that *property is divided just once, but career assets continue to produce income regularly for years.*

The courts assume equal independence from both partners. Sometimes the court will award rehabilitative maintenance to ease a spouse into the work force. But the courts base these settlements on the assumption — often false — that both spouses can be equally self-sufficient. In reality, *marriage creates economic inequality.*

> **In creating an equitable financial settlement, it is important to remember that property is divided just once, but career assets continue to produce income regularly for years.**

Research on divorce has found that the most important issue to women is financial survival. They are terrified of becoming "bag ladies!" Yet this fear isn't as irrational or emotion-based as it may sound. In the late 1980s, several states set up task forces to study gender bias in the courts. For example, in Colorado, one section of the task force was charged with the area of divorce. This section studied cases taken directly from the court files. The parameters were that (1) the marriage had lasted 12 years or longer, (2) the case be decided by a judge as opposed to being settled out of court (the task force wanted to see the results of what the judges were doing), and (3) there was a minimum of $10,000 in positive net worth.[1]

Findings included:

- Out of 28 cases, the average length of marriage was 20.5 years.
- At the time of divorce, the average age of the wife was 44, the husband's 45.
- 11 of the 28 families had net assets of less than $50,000 at the time of divorce and 10 had net assets of $100,000 or more.[2]

Figure 1–1 illustrates the results of this study. It is a composite of the 28 cases, showing the average net worth of husband and wife at the time of the divorce (based on the court-ordered property division) and the projected change in net worth for each of them. At the time of the court order, the wife's average net worth is slightly greater than the husband's, because she is usually allocated less of the marital debt. Within four years of the divorce, however, the wife's projected net worth *declines* by 25 percent while the husband's nearly doubles. Within eight years of the divorce, the wife will have a negative net worth while the husband's projected net worth is approximately $200,000.[3]

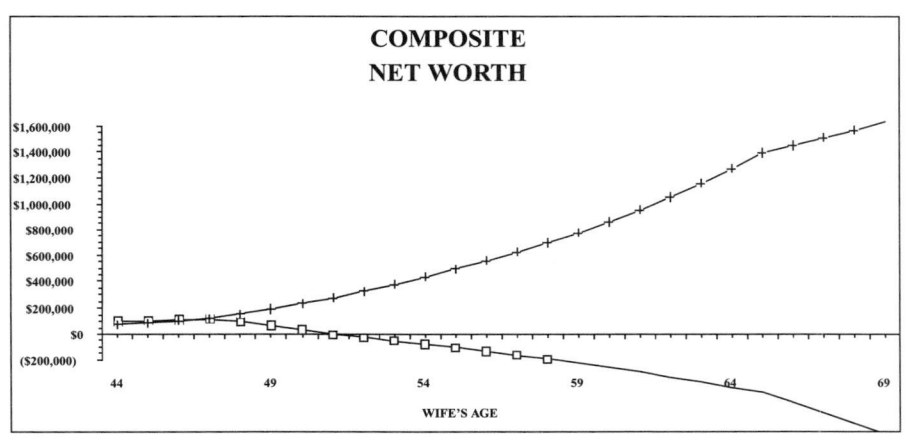

Figure 1–1   COMPOSITE NET WORTH
This composite, based on 28 case studies, illustrates the average net worth of the husband and the wife at the time of divorce (based on the court-ordered property division) and the projected change in net worth for each of them.

Besides looking at the court files, the Colorado task force also interviewed a number of divorced men and women. One interviewed woman told her story about the maintenance award she received after *38 years of marriage* during which she was not employed. The judge ordered her husband to pay her $300 per month for two years. He awarded the house, appraised at $160,000, to the wife, and all the other assets, including a retirement fund, to the husband, saying, "Mother has been out of the work force, and if we gave her all that money she wouldn't know how to handle it."[4]

Another interviewed woman told the Colorado task force that she had been awarded a tractor as part of the property settlement but her ex-husband refused to deliver it. She had tried for four years without success to get the original order enforced. One district judge even gave her former husband permission to continue using the tractor. When her lawyer objected, the judge asked her what she was going to do with the tractor.[5]

> **The Washington State Task Force on Gender and Justice in the Courts found that only 10% of all wives being divorced were awarded maintenance, and the average amount was $432 per month for an average length of 2.6 years. The national average as of spring 1986 had 15% of wives receiving an average of $329 per month.[6]**

A 1997 report from the Business and Professional Women's Foundation has gathered together the following statistics:

1. The average woman loses approximately $420,000 over a lifetime due to unequal pay practices.
2. Women on average can expect to live 19 years into retirement while men can expect to live 15 years.
3. Only 39% of all working women and fewer than 17% of part-time working women are covered by a pension plan.
4. Only 20% of all widows receive a survivor pension, which is usually only 50% of what their husband's benefits had been.
5. Fewer than one-fourth of divorced women age 62 and older receive any employer sponsored pension income, whether from their own or their ex-husband's past work. Often, divorced women are left with no share of their ex-husband's pension, even after a long marriage.
6. In 1995, women comprised only 58% of the total elderly population but comprised 74% of the elderly poor. Older women are twice as likely as older men to be poor, and nearly 40% of older women living alone live in or near poverty level.
7. Of all unmarried women age 65 and older, 40% rely on Social Security for 90% or more of their household income.
8. The U.S. has the greatest percentage of elderly women in poverty of all the major industrialized nations.

HIS SIDE: THE VICTIM

The awakening of the men's movement in the U.S. has provided significant insight into the pain and emotion that men experience. The divorce process is a common source for much of that pain. Surprisingly, in many cases it is the man — not the woman — who is paralyzed by emotions. Feeling terribly victimized, men tend to conclude that courts agree with the cynical saying, "What's his is theirs and what's hers is hers."

Men have several very real concerns. The number one concern for fathers with young children is how the divorce will affect their relationship with their children. Even though we hear about fathers who abandon their children after divorce, this is not the prevailing behavior. During divorce, men fight for the right to participate in the lives of their children. Only if denied that right do they sometimes walk away in frustration and discontinue child support payments.

Fathers dread their lack of control in the divorce situation and fear the court's power to decree the most intimate details of their relationship with children. The fact that a man and woman no longer get along with each other does not mean that a father loves his children less. In fact, in many cases going through a divorce takes the father through an educational process that brings him closer to his own hidden emotions — paving the way towards a warmer and more participative role as a dad.

After the issue of children, another foremost concern is the prospect of paying life-time alimony to his ex-wife. No one wants to be tied into that possibility. Men want an end to the payments. They believe they cannot get on with their own lives as long as they have to pay out a large portion of their income to someone who is no longer a part of their life. They see this as keeping the relationship going with no possibility of relief. They really do not understand why, when a relationship is at an end, they should have an obligation to support this person indefinitely. Their need for closure is strong.

Having to pay out large sums in the first few years after a divorce for things like child support, alimony, attorney's fees (both his and hers), as well as property settlement, means that a man's discretionary income may suffer greatly. He frequently feels that he has been "taken to the cleaners" and that he is doomed to pay for the divorce forever. In some cases, he may be right. But statistics show that in the vast majority of cases, the financial effects of divorce are relatively short-lived. Men can take solace in the fact that their earning potential is almost always higher than their soon to be ex-wife's and they will eventually be financially better off than she.

A critical concern to men is sharing their pensions. The husband feels he has earned the pension and, therefore, he should not have to share it with anyone. It's interesting that, in many cases, the man will agree to a 50/50 property split and give the wife other assets in exchange for keeping his pension - "just don't touch my pension!" It becomes an extremely emotional issue that can steer a man in the wrong direction!

For the self-employed man, his main concern is his business. If it has significant value, this can be an area of great concern for both sides. All too often it is the only asset of real value and since it cannot be divided, paying the wife her half of the value can be a real problem.

A universal concern is the perception that the deck is stacked against men from the start due to pressures applied from a press sympathetic towards women. Men feel that they are made to pay the price for a minority of husbands and fathers who do ignore their responsibilities. It is the experience of many men that they are "assumed guilty" for the breakup of the marriage — and that they must pay in order to atone for this sin.

During their research, the Colorado task force received complaints from men who felt they had indeed been victims of gender bias in awards of spousal maintenance or child support. As one man stated, "The purpose of maintenance is to sustain the weaker of the parties, when that one has contributed to the rise of the union by sacrifice of career or education, until such time that the weaker one becomes established and self-sufficient. In my case, the wife was the direct cause of the financial problems of the union and should not be rewarded for that. This lady has no intention to re-train or have a career."[7]

IS AN EQUITABLE DIVORCE SETTLEMENT POSSIBLE?

There's no denying that divorce often has a devastating impact on everyone involved. While some couples effect a "civilized" divorce and can remain cordial, most couples go to battle, especially if they end up in court, leading to a permanently damaging result on the rest of their lives.

As we discussed earlier, can something really be done to lessen the negative impact of divorce? Are equitable settlements really possible? Yes.

However, few judges and attorneys are financial experts. Financial analysis of the outcome of possible settlements is complex and requires substantial experience. When legal expertise is not matched with sophisticated financial projections, an apparently equal division of property can leave the lower- or non-earning spouse destitute within a few years.

Contrary to popular belief, arranging a settlement that benefits the lower-earning spouse does not necessarily have to harm the higher-earning spouse. In addition, even though a lower standard of living may be anticipated, it does not have to be dramatically lowered for either spouse.

Although it is impossible to predict the future, sophisticated software methodology can be used to forecast the eventual financial outcome of specific divorce settlements. Such software allows judges, lawyers, and divorcing couples to compare the outcome of various suggested settlements. The DivorceCalc™ software program can be used to test different scenarios, such as higher or longer lasting maintenance, disproportionate property division, and reduced standards of living.

Armed with available software and knowledgeable professionals well versed in the intricacies of putting together equitable final settlements and experts dedicated to helping couples avoid the court battle, a more humane result can be accomplished.

This book helps to strip away the sensational biases to provide the tools necessary to equip both spouses with the education and clarity needed but often difficult to find when faced with a looming divorce.

Getting Started

- Gather information! Many times one spouse is handling a given task concerning loan applications or investments, while the other spouse may not know about the ongoings of this task. Get informed. Gather as much information as possible. Every piece of the puzzle will help you to generate a complete picture.

- Get copies of everything! It's amazing how quickly documents can disappear once a divorce is decided upon. Trying to get copies of these documents after the fact through your lawyer is timely and costly.
- Save up! Once you think that divorce is on the horizon, start saving away as much cash as you can. You will need to hire professionals to help you through this and that is going to cost money!
- Lastly, prepare detailed expense reports. Financials are the most argued about area in divorce proceedings — in fact, it may even be the crux of your divorce! Be sure to make copies of check registers and credit card statements to support and provide evidence for high expenses in certain areas. (Sample forms can be found in the Appendix to assist you with this process.)

Notes

1. Colorado Supreme Court Task Force on Gender Bias In The Courts. 1990.
2. Colorado Supreme Court Task Force on Gender Bias In The Courts. 1990.
3. Colorado Supreme Court Task Force on Gender Bias In The Courts. 1990.
4. Colorado Supreme Court Task Force on Gender Bias In The Courts. 1990.
5. Colorado Supreme Court Task Force on Gender Bias In The Courts. 1990.
6. Washington State Task Force on Gender and Justice In The Courts. 1989.
7. Colorado Supreme Court Task Force on Gender Bias In The Courts. 1990.

PART 2

THE DIVISION –
NOT ALL 50/50
SPLITS ARE
EQUITABLE

chapter 2

PROPERTY: VALUATIONS AND SETTLEMENTS

During her marriage, Joyce's husband had done all of the investing on their behalf. He had chosen all of the investments, made all of financial related decisions, and invested all their money.

At divorce time, he said, "Let's just split everything 50/50. You take this half of the investments and I'll take that half. Is that okay?"

Not having been involved in the overall investments during their marriage, Joyce said, "Well, I guess that sounds pretty fair. Sure, that's okay with me."

After her divorce, Joyce went to a financial planner to see how to best reposition her assets. Together, they decided to do a total financial plan for her. Unfortunately, there was something she did not know or understand when agreeing to the "50/50" split. Neither did her attorney nor the judge. What no one realized was that Joyce was getting the half of the investments with *all* the limited partnerships. Her "50/50" split ended up costing her an additional *$18,000* in taxes!

Had Joyce seen a financial planner *before* the divorce was final, she would have been in a much better position to formulate a more equitable settlement.

Sound familiar? Most families these days tend to divvy up the household chores such as paying the bills, mowing the lawn, or going to the grocery store. Inevitably, the chore of investing the family's savings tends to still fall on the shoulders of one spouse or the other. All too often, while the non-investing spouse may be aware of the family's overall investment decisions, they are not well versed on the day-to-day details. So how can you protect yourself? How can you be sure that the split offered truly is a 50/50 split?

Let's begin with dividing your property. When looking at the property issues in divorce, you should always ask the following three questions:

1. What is defined as marital property?
2. What is it worth?
3. How will it be divided?

In addition to those items traditionally seen as property, don't forgot to take into consideration career assets. Remember: After the divorce is final, you can't go back and change your mind about how something was divided up.

Although each situation is different, there are some generalities when it comes to the type of property jointly owned by couples. "Most divorcing couples have household furnishings (89%), cars (71%), and some savings in the form of money in bank accounts, stocks, or bonds (61%). Almost half (46%) of the couples own or are buying a family home, which is likely to be a couple's most valuable asset. Only a small proportion of divorcing couples have a pension (24%), a business (11%), or other real estate (11%)."[1]

It has been said that most divorcing couples have a net worth of less than $20,000. If this is so, it may be that couples are investing in their careers and earning capabilities instead of increasing their savings accounts. They may see their careers as being more valuable than tangible assets. Because future income is typically of greater value than property, the main financial issues at divorce, particularly for women and children, are those of spousal and child support.

> **Transferred property between husband and wife is not taxable.**

WHAT IS DEFINED AS MARITAL PROPERTY?

Property includes such assets as the family home, rental property, cars, and art or antique collections. It can also include bank accounts, mutual funds, stocks and bonds, life insurance cash value, IRAs, and retirement plans. As you can see, there is virtually no limit to what can be considered property.

Be aware that the state you reside in also affects what is defined as marital property. In some states, regardless of how property was brought to the marriage or who has title, all property of both spouses is subject to division and disposition at divorce. These states do not differentiate between marital and non-marital (or separate) property. However, the "source" of the property (gift, inheritance, owned prior to marriage, etc.), while ignored when classifying the property, may be very important in the way in which the property is divided.

Although the laws vary from state to state, property in most states is usually divided into just two categories: separate and marital (sometimes called "community") property. In general, separate property includes what a person

  a. brings into the marriage
  b. inherits during the marriage
  c. receives as a gift during the marriage.

On the other hand, marital property is everything acquired during the marriage no matter whose name it's in.

In most states, separate property is everything you bring into the marriage and keep in your own name. It is also what you received during the marriage as a gift or an inheritance. Martial property is everything that has been acquired during the marriage – no matter whose name it's in.

To give you a better idea of the various types of property and how they are defined, let's review a few examples. For instance, Beth and her husband Ryan are getting a divorce. They currently live in a state where both marital and separate property is recognized. When they got married, Beth had $1,000 in a savings account. During the marriage, her $1,000 earned $100 in interest and now the account is worth $1,100.

Her property is defined as $1,000, because she kept it in her name only, and in some states, the $100 in interest goes into the pot of marital assets to be divided because that is the increase in value of her separate property. However, if Beth had put her husband's name on the account, she would have turned the entire account into a marital asset. She would have made a presumptive gift to the marriage.

In second or third marriages, it is likely that both people may bring a house into the marriage. Taking the example from above, suppose that Beth had a house when she got married, but decided to keep it in her name only. At that time, the house was worth $100,000 and had a mortgage on it of $70,000, so the equity was $30,000. Now, Beth is getting divorced. Today the house is worth $150,000. The mortgage is down to about $50,000. Equity has since increased to $100,000.

	Value	Mortgage	Equity
At Marriage	$100,000.00	$(70,000.00)	$ 30,000.00
At Divorce	$150,000.00	$(50,000.00)	$100,000.00

The increase in value is due to the increase in the equity or $70,000.

Let's reverse the situation. Assume Beth put Ryan's name on the deed to the house when they got married. After all, they were going to be together for the rest of their lives. As soon as she put his name on the deed, she gave what is called a "presumptive gift" to the marriage, thus turning the house into a marital asset.

Now, let's assume that Beth's aunt died and left her $10,000. That is considered an inheritance. If she was to put it into an account with only her name on it, then at the time of divorce, it is her separate property minus the increase in value. It is the same with a gift. If she received a gift of $10,000 and put it into a joint account, Beth would have turned that money into marital property.

Beth saves $100 of her paycheck every month. She puts this $100 a month into an account with her name only, and now it is worth $2,600. At the time of their divorce, would this money be considered separate or marital property? It is marital property since it was acquired during the marriage, no matter whose name it's in.

When Beth got married, Ryan gave her an eight-carat diamond ring. Let's assume that they are in court and she is testifying that the ring was a gift from him so it is her separate property. Ryan says, "Are you kidding? I would not give you an eight-carat diamond. That was an investment. Therefore, it is marital property." It is for the judge to decide.

What if Ryan had given her an $80,000 painting for her birthday? Beth claimed it was a gift and he claimed it was an investment and, therefore, should be treated as marital property. The judge could consider it an investment. Since it is not the type of thing that most people would freely give as a gift, it could be seen as an investment for the family, therefore, considered marital property. But remember: You can never predict what the judge will decide.

HOW WILL PROPERTY BE DIVIDED WHEN YOU BOTH WANT THE SAME ITEM?

The above examples are fairly straightforward in explaining what constitutes as property — but what happens when both parties want the same item? How is your property divided then?

Beth and Ryan had divided all their property except for one item. They couldn't agree upon who was going to get the set of antique crystal that they had purchased in England. The result? They both wanted it so badly that they ended up spending an additional $60,000 in court fees to decide that one issue. At $60,000, they could have each flown to England and bought a set! This may seem absurd, but it happens every day.

More often then not, the home furnishings and general household goods such as the above set of antique crystal are not included on the list of assets because most couples simply divide the items. However, if a given item is to be valued, the typical value is what you *could* get *if* the items were sold at a garage sale or on eBay. The exceptions would be antiques, art, collections, etc. in which case an appraisal may be needed if either of you feel that there is great value to them. For example, autos are typically valued by their Blue Book value.

LOCATION, LOCATION, LOCATION!

What kind of state do you live in? That is, what rules of property and labeling does your state follow? When buying a house, we all will consider the crime rate of our area or how good the school systems are, but how many of us ever stop to consider the type of state we live in? When on the threshold of finalizing your divorce, it can be a critical component in your final settlement split.

There are mostly two different types of states — community property states and equitable distribution states — and be warned: the differences are subtle. Although the technicalities of how your state handles the division are best left to the professionals, it is important to understand the difference between the two when reviewing which property is yours, your spouse's, or yours as a "couple."

Community property states: First, identify the property that is not subject to division of the court, which is the husband's and wife's separate property. The husband's or wife's "separate property" generally is owned before the marriage or obtained by gift or inheritance. Everything else is "community property" and is subject to a 50/50 division. When in doubt, the state presumes the property is owned by the "community." Any property acquired in a community property state retains its community property status, no matter where the couple moves.

Equitable distribution states, on the other hand, usually agree that the couple's property — "marital property" — is divided between the husband and wife *equitably* or fairly. It is important to note that this does not necessarily mean 50/50.

MARTHA AND TOM

Martha and Tom have been married for 35 years. She stayed home and took care of their four children. Tom earns $150,000 per year and has started a business in the basement of their home. He expects the new business will bring in revenues after he retires. They own their home, which is worth $135,000; it is completely paid off. His pension has been valued at $90,000. Their savings account is $28,000, and Tom values the basement business at $75,000. Their assets total $328,000. Assuming a 50/50 property split, each would receive $164,000.

These are their assets:

House	$135,000
Pension	$90,000
Savings	$28,000
Business	$75,000
Total	$328,000

However, splitting the property and assets down the middle is often *not* the most equitable division, as this example will illustrate. Martha wants the house. As a homemaker, she has raised their four children and has a strong emotional attachment to it. (*A note of caution: You may have agreed upon the value of your home, but what if Martha was to get it but was then forced to sell it and was only able to get $95,000? She would have left $40,000 on the settlement table!*)

While women often have an emotional attachment to the house, men tend to have emotional attachments to their pension. Tom is no exception. He has also requested their savings account. He has a business deal coming up and is going to need the additional cash flow.

Tom goes on to request the entire business. Since Martha has never set foot in there and hasn't shared in this venture of his, she doesn't disagree.

Based on the above, here's what the property settlement breakout looks like:

	Pre-Divorce	**Martha**	**Tom**
House	$135,000.00	$135,000.00	
Pension	$ 90,000.00		$ 90,000.00
Savings	$ 28,000.00		$ 28,000.00
Business	$ 75,000.00		$ 75,000.00
Total	**$328,000.00**	**$135,000.00**	**$193,000.00**

Martha's total assets equal $135,000 and Tom's assets total $193,000. If we were to look at a 50/50 property split, he would owe her $29,000. Although Tom has a large income of $150,000 a year, he doesn't want to give up any of the business, pension or savings.

So what are his options? They could choose to even out this division with a Property Settlement Note. Tom can pay Martha $29,000 over time, like a note at the bank. He can make monthly payments with current market interest. Or, he can borrow funds directly from the bank, since he has assets, including a savings account comparable to what he would owe.

> A Property Settlement Note is from the payer to the payee for an agreed-upon length of time with reasonable interest. It is still considered division of property, so the payer does not deduct it from taxable income. The payee does not pay taxes on the principal – only on the interest. It is important to collateralize this note.

But Martha doesn't like this settlement. "I want the house and I want half of your pension. We have been married for 35 years and I helped you earn that pension." Place the house ($135,000) in her column and add $45,000 of the pension in her column and subtract $45,000 from Tom's column. Then she says, "I want half of the savings account. You are not going to leave me without any cash." Put $14,000 in her column and subtract $14,000 from Tom's column. She agrees that the business is Tom's, so the $75,000 is left in his column.

Their property split now looks like this:

	Pre-Divorce	Martha	Tom
House	$135,000.00	$135,000.00	
Pension	$ 90,000.00	$ 45,000.00	$ 45,000.00
Savings	$ 28,000.00	$ 14,000.00	$ 14,000.00
Business	$ 75,000.00		$ 75,000.00
Total	$328,000.00	$194,000.00	$134,000.00

Her assets are valued at $194,000, his at $134,000. Martha owes Tom $30,000 to make an equal 50/50 property settlement. Yet, it's not that simple. She doesn't have a job, has arthritis, and cannot walk very well. In reality, Martha is not in good health and it is unlikely she would be able to get a job that pays much above the minimum wage.

Her largest asset is the house, an illiquid asset. It is paid for, but it does not create revenue to buy groceries. She could rent out rooms for additional income, but that rarely works and it creates a different lifestyle that she may not want. How is she going to pay $30,000 to Tom? The prospects are bleak. Given that Martha is in her mid-50s, has never worked outside the home, and her largest asset is illiquid, they may decide that this unequal division may be considered the most equitable in the end.

DIVIDING MARITAL PROPERTY AND DEBTS

The above exercise of listing per person the asset wished to keep is helpful in "seeing" the balance or lack thereof. Questions to ask yourself as you are making your list:

- Are you more interested in cash than in things?
- Are you willing to accept less than 50% if your share is all cash?
- Are you more interested in future security than in present assets?
- Would you be interested in a "lopsided" agreement to compensate for the larger earnings of either you or your spouse?

You want to think beyond the short-term to the long-term effect of the decisions you are making on the division of assets and debts. For example, suppose you decide you want the home, car, and all of the furniture. These are all assets that appreciate slowly or in some cases depreciate and, just as important, require money to maintain. Suppose your spouse agreed and took any stock, retirement accounts, or rental homes that you had? These are all assets that either increase in value or are income producing. What might seem fair now in the short-term, may look quite different in the long-term.

CAREER ASSETS

As was the case with "Martha and Tom" and is often with most couples, one spouse has significant assets tied to his or her career. These career assets include:

- Life insurance
- Health insurance
- Disability insurance
- Vacation pay
- Sick pay
- Social Security benefits
- Unemployment benefits
- Stock options
- Pension plans
- Retirement savings plans
- Promotions

- Job experience
- Seniority
- Professional contacts
- Education

For example, let's take a family in which the husband is the sole wage earner as was the case with Martha and Tom. Many times, the wife put the husband through school or helped him become established. At the same time, she may have abandoned or postponed her own education in the process. She may have quit her job to move from job to job with him or to stay at home to raise their family. Together, they have made the decision to spend the time and energy to build his career with the understanding that she will share in the fruits of her investment through her husband's enhanced earning power. Over time, he has built up career assets that are part of what he earns, even though they may not be paid out directly to him.

Even in two-income families, one spouse's career (usually the husband's) takes priority. Both spouses expect to share the rewards of that decision. At least, in the beginning of their marriage. Some states even place a value on degrees such as the medical degree, the dental degree, or the law degree.

There was an interesting case in 1998 that involved Lorna and Gary Wendt. It was a highly publicized battle over career assets that even made the cover of *Fortune* magazine. He was the CEO of GE Capital, she was a "corporate wife."

The Wendts, married shortly after both graduated from the University of Wisconsin, began their life with a net worth of $2,500. She gave up her job as a music teacher after her husband graduated from Harvard Business School. Lorna's Ph.T., or "Putting Hubby Through" degree, was introduced as evidence at the divorce proceedings.

At the time of divorce, he declared the marital estate to be worth $21 million and offered her $8 million as her share. She argued that the estate was worth $100 million and she wanted half — $50 million. Her position was that his future pension benefits and stock options had been earned during their marriage. She said that her contribution as the homemaker and wife of the CEO enabled him to rise through the ranks to the top of his organization.

The Wendt case broke through the long-held belief that "enough is enough" — that a spouse deserved enough to maintain their lifestyle — nothing more. In a landmark decision, the judge awarded her $20 million — far less than the $50 million she asked for, but far more than the $8 million her husband initially offered. She also received $250,000 per year in alimony!

THE FAMILY BUSINESS

In the Tom and Martha case, Tom was just beginning his own business. But what happens when the business is a long-term endeavor that both partners have been involved in creating? Whenever one of the marital assets in a divorce is a business, there are challenges in dividing this asset. A business can be anything from dentistry, medicine or law, to real estate, or a home-based business. It can be a sole proprietorship, a partnership, or a corporation.

VALUE THE BUSINESS

There are a multitude of fears, non-stronger then your financial stability. However, **it is critical that an appraisal of the family business be done.** Admittedly, it is a complicated and costly process but it will empower you to make an informed decision regarding your share of the final settlement.

Let's look at the case of Becky and James. After 35 years of marriage, they were getting a divorce. James owned a heavy construction business. He agreed to split the assets 50/50 and said that the CPA at work had valued the business at $300,000. Becky told her attorney, "I used to keep the books in the business for James when we first started out and I know we took in more than a million dollars each year. Do you think it would only be worth $300,000?"

Fortunately, Becky's attorney insisted that she have the business appraised. The appraisal cost Becky $4,300, which made her very nervous to spend so much money. But the appraisal valued the company at $850,000 so her investment of $4,300 netted her $275,000 more than she would have received with the $300,000 valuation!

DIVIDING THE BUSINESS

There are three options when deciding how to divide the business. Either you or your spouse keeps the business, both of you keep the business, or you sell the business outright.

Option 1: One Spouse Keeps the Business

This is the most common solution and tends to work the best for most couples.

In Becky and James' case, it was pretty clear that James ran the business and, having such a vested interest, he would want to keep the business and buy out Becky's interest or give her other assets of equal value.

Option 2: Both Continue to Work in the Business

On the other hand, it is much more difficult to divide a family owned business where the husband and wife have worked next to each other every day for years. They both have emotional and financial ties with the business. In addition, if they try to divide the business, it may kill the business. Some couples are better business partners than marriage partners, and are able to continue to work together in a business even after the divorce is final. However, this won't work for everyone!

Option 3: Sell the Business

Another option is to sell the business and divide the profits. This way, both parties are free to look elsewhere for another business or even to retire. The problem here may be in finding a buyer. It sometimes takes years to sell a business. In the meantime, until the business is sold, decisions need to be made as to whose business it is and who runs it.

HIDDEN ASSET CHECKLIST

The divorce process is a time of mistrust for each spouse, and, right or wrong, each may accuse the other of hiding assets. Although the research of hidden assets is best left in the hands of a professional attorney (see appendix for a complete list of resources as well as paperwork you may be asked for), it is important for you to be aware that they may exist and where. Assets are traditionally hidden in one of four ways. The person either

1. denies the existence of an asset
2. transfers it to a third party
3. or claims the asset was lost or dissipated.

In addition to these, there is a new way to hide assets:

4. creation of false debt.

It is the attorney's responsibility to organize and coordinate discovery. However, he or she may ask for your assistance.

Summary

- Property settlement is a done deal! After the divorce is final, it is too late to change your mind about how something was divided.
- Know the difference between separate and marital property. Check with your own state to see how property is handled or ask your lawyer.
- Get both your real estate and your family business appraised! You may agree on the value of your home or business but it is quite possible you're leaving substantial sums of money on the settlement table. Hire the experts who will provide you with the necessary information to make an informed decision about your final settlement.
- Remember, household goods are valued at garage sale or eBay value. Household goods include furniture, pots and pans, sheets, towels, etc. Exceptions to this are antiques, art, collections etc. However, don't hesitate to get an item appraised if you feel there is greater value to it.
- Long-term value vs. short-term value: Sometimes, assets come in later, after the divorce is final such as a bonus or tax refunds — be sure to include them in today's settlement. Evaluate your settlement options and be conscious of your needs today as well as in the future.

Notes

1. *The Divorce Revolution* by Lenore Weitzman, Chapter 3: "The Nature of Marital Property," The Free Press (A Division of Macmillan, Inc.), 1985.

WHO GETS THE HOUSE?

When Karen and Todd got divorced, Karen took the house, which had equity of $90,000 and Todd took the 401(k). Alimony was paid to Karen for three years and when it stopped, she realized she could not keep up with such high house payments, so she put the house up for sale. The real estate market was in a downward spin and Karen had to keep dropping the asking price on the house. She finally sold it for a little more than the mortgage balance. Her $90,000 asset from the marriage had completely evaporated.

As we discussed in the last chapter, dividing your property can be one of the most challenging and convoluted aspects of your divorce. What appears to be an easy decision such as I want the house, you keep the cars, may in the end deliver you a settlement you hadn't bargained for. As we illustrated in the above example, not only did Karen lose the house that she had much more then just money invested in, she also lost the one asset she had regained from the end of her marriage.

In many divorces, the biggest question is: Who gets the house? Should the wife get it? Should the husband? Or should they sell it and split the profit (if there is one)? Oftentimes, the answer isn't easy or clear.

Many times, the wife has an emotional tie to the house and wants to keep it. This is where she raised the children, decorated, and entertained. Her whole married life has revolved around this house. There is a certain safety and comfort that she finds in the familiarity of the house. Unfortunately, she does not stop to think about the value of that asset. If it is almost paid off and has a lot of equity in it, she is getting an illiquid asset that does not buy groceries for her and her children, nor does it generate any income.

THREE BASIC OPTIONS

There are three basic options available to couples when approaching the issue of who gets the house:

1. Sell the house.
2. Have one spouse buy out the other spouse's interest in the over-all property settlement.
3. Have both ex-spouses continue to own the property jointly.

SELL THE HOUSE

Selling the house and dividing the profits that remain after sales costs and the mortgage is paid off is the easiest and "cleanest" way both emotionally and financially of dividing equity. Concerns that you will need to address include: the basis and possible capital gains (dealt with later in this chapter), buying another house vs. renting, and being able to qualify for a new loan.

BUY OUT THE OTHER SPOUSE

Buying out your spouse's interest works if one person wants to remain in the house or wants to own the house, but there are difficulties with this option that you'll need to consider.

First of all, a value of the property needs to be agreed to. (I would also recommend that you get the house appraised by a professional, just to be on the safe side.) Next, you'll need to decide on the dollar amount of the buyout. Will the dollar amount have to be subtracted from its selling costs and capital gains taxes (in case the owner needs to sell it sooner than expected)?

There may be other assets that can go to the spouse who surrenders the house. If there are inadequate assets, a method of payment needs to be selected. If there is a time period to pay the other spouse, the terms need to be comfortable for both parties. The house could be refinanced to withdraw cash to pay the other spouse, or a note payable can be drawn up with terms of payment agreeable to both parties. In the case of a note, there should be reasonable interest attached to it and it should be collateralized with a deed of trust on the property. A problem with this arrangement is that it keeps you and your ex-spouse in an uncomfortable debtor-creditor relationship.

There is another problem with buying out the your spouse's interest. Let's say the wife gets the house and both names are on the deed. The husband can quitclaim the deed to her so that only her name is on the deed. She can sell it whenever she wants to. Although his name comes off the deed, it remains on the mortgage. He is still liable if she decided to quit making the payments. The mortgage company most likely will not care if they are divorced or not, and will probably refuse to "release" the other spouse. The only way he can get his name off the mortgage may be for her to assume the loan, refinance it or pay it off. When the husband's name is kept on the mortgage, this may impact his credit. He could be viewed as overextended, unless he has proof that she is making the mortgage payments. This continues what may be an adversarial relationship.

OWN THE HOUSE JOINTLY

The last option — continuing to own the property jointly — is one often used by some couples when they want the children to stay in the house until they finish school, reach a certain age or the resident ex-spouse remarries or cohabits.

You may agree to sell the house after your children have graduated from school and split the proceeds evenly. Perhaps you even agree that the one who stays in the house in the meantime can pay the mortgage payment while all other costs of maintaining the house plus taxes and repairs can be split evenly. Again, this creates a financial tie between you and your ex-spouse that may create stress.

To help put all these options into perspective, let's review some examples:

Mark and Susan both held very good jobs when they decided to divorce in 1986. Susan wanted to stay in the house with the three children and buy out Mark's half of the house with a property settlement note. Interest rates were high. The note was drawn with her agreeing to pay him his half of the equity at 14 percent interest. Then, property values began to decline. Susan's half of the equity was losing value, his half was earning 14 percent, even after the interest rates plummeted.

Nobody presumed at the time they drew up this agreement that interest rates or property values were going to go down.

It is always a risk when you do agreements that extend out into the future.

It is important to keep both short-term and long-term values in mind when finalizing your settlement. A good general rule of thumb to keep in mind is: If the discussion is about dividing assets prior to a year, specifying hard dollars usually works. But further in the future, it is much safer and much wiser to talk percentages.

DETERMINING THE BASIS

After being involved with over 1,000 divorce cases, I am still amazed at the numerous times the basis in the house was not discussed when determining its value. I find that the one question most overlooked by attorneys is: "What is the basis in this asset (assets including stocks, real estate, or other investments in the couple's portfolio)?"

Let's take a look at an example that will illustrate how important the basis of an asset can be when determining its value: June and Stan are getting divorced and they have three assets: a cabin on a lake worth $190,000, a 401(k) plan worth $90,000 and a Certificate of Deposit (CD) worth $140,000. Stan said, "Why don't you take the cabin and sell it?" He had borrowed $140,000 against the cabin a year before and put the money into a CD, which she was aware of. "If you sell it, you will get $50,000. You take the 401(k) worth $90,000, and I'll take the CD, so we each end up with $140,000."

June talked this over with her attorney and they thought that this sounded fair.

	Assets	June	Stan
Cabin	$ 190,000.00		
	$ (140,000.00)		
Total Assumed Value	$ 50,000.00	$ 50,000.00	
401(k)	$ 90,000.00	$ 90,000.00	
CD	$ 140,000.00		$140,000.00
Total	$ 280,000.00	$140,000.00	$140,000.00

What Stan did not talk about — and what the attorney *should* have asked about — was the basis in the cabin. Stan had paid $20,000 for this cabin 15 years earlier. There was a $170,000 capital gain, which created a tax of $42,500 (capital gains tax at 15% plus state tax at 5%). June did indeed receive $50,000 but had to turn around and pay out $34,000, leaving her with only $16,000!

Capital gain	$170,000.00
Federal tax (15%)	$ 25,500.00
State tax (5%)	$ 8,500.00
Total capital gains tax	$ 34,000.00

The after-tax value of the 401(k) plan is approximately $60,300, so June ends up with a total settlement of $76,300. The $140,000 that Stan borrowed from the cabin and put in the CD was his, tax-free and clear. He ends up with $140,000 and she with $76,300, because the question was not asked about the basis. Do you think June's attorney had some liability here? Absolutely!

	Assets	June	Stan
Cabin	$ 16,000.00	$ 16,000.00	
401(k)	$ 60,300.00	$ 60,300.00	
CD	$ 140,000.00		$140,000.00
Total	**$ 216,300.00**	**$ 76,300.00**	**$140,000.00**

Another question that couples often need to be aware of and consider when determining the basis is what is considered a home improvement? While maintenance costs don't increase the tax basis of the home, improvements do. If you have spent a substantial amount of money on improvements, you'll want to make a list of improvements to give to your attorney or accountant to review.

TAX IMPLICATION ISSUES ON THE SALE OF YOUR HOME

In divorce, your most valuable asset is often times your house. Questions arise as to whether to sell it or keep it. The tax implications of these questions are usually overlooked until well after the divorce. As a result, the sale of the home can create an unforeseen income tax liability. In 1997, the Tax Relief Act 1997 (TRA '97) was passed stating that we could no longer roll over capital gain in the family home. The one time exclusion of $125,000 is also gone. However, what was provided for us is much better!

Now, each spouse can take up to $250,000 exclusion if you have lived in the house for two of the past five years. This means that it is possible for both you and your ex-spouse to take the $250,000 exclusion for a total of $500,000 if it is handled properly. (Make sure you consult with a CPA or Financial Divorce Specialist to help you take advantage of the new tax laws and regulations.)

The Old Tax Law Prior to Tax Relief Act 1997 (TRA '97) Said:

- We could rollover our gain into a house of equal or greater value without realizing capital gains.
- We could take a one time $125,000 exclusion from capital gain after age 55.
- Our capital gains were taxed at 28%.

Our New Exclusions Allowed Under TRA '97 Include:

- Single taxpayers can exclude $250,000 from capital gains.
- Married filing jointly can exclude $500,000 from capital gains.
- These exclusions are allowed for one sale every 2 years.

The New Tax Rates Are:

- 15% maximum for taxpayers in upper brackets.
- 10% for taxpayers in the 15% bracket.

Let's look at some examples:

1. John and Mary are getting divorced. John is awarded the jointly owned family home but agrees to pay 50% of all profits to Mary upon selling it. At the end of four years, John decides to sell the home and 50% of the proceeds are sent to Mary as agreed upon.

   Tax Implications:

   Scenario A: John sells the home for $400,000. Mary will receive $200,000 and be entitled to use her $250,000 exclusion even though she has not lived in the home for the previous four years.

   Scenario B: John sells the home for $750,000. Mary will receive $375,000. If the basis in the property was $100,000, Mary's portion of the basis is $50,000 leaving her with a $325,000 gain. Even though she uses her $250,000 exclusion, she will be taxed on the remaining $75,000 of gain.

$750,000 Sales price	$750,000 Sales price
$100,000 Basis	$375,000 John's half
$650,000 Capital Gain	$375,000 Mary's half

$375,000	Mary's half of Sales Price
−$ 50,000	Mary's half of Basis
$325,000	Mary's half of Capital Gain
−$250,000	Mary's Exclusion
$ 75,000	Amount Mary will be taxed on

But sometimes the new rule is not so advantageous. Look at the case of Vickie.

2. Vickie is getting divorced and it has been decided that she will take the house valued at $750,000. The basis in the house is $200,000. Vickie decides to move to another city. Remembering the old rule that in order to escape taxes, she must buy a house of equal or greater value, Vickie buys another house for $750,000. Her gain on the sale is $550,000. Vickie will be able to use her $250,000 exclusion but will still have to pay taxes on the gain of $300,000 even though she bought another house of equal value! **(Remember, the rollover is a thing of the past.)**

$750,000	Sales price
−$200,000	Basis
$550,000	Capital gain
−$250,000	Exclusion
$300,000	Amount Vickie will be taxed on

One good thing that the new tax law gave us is that this is not a one-time exclusion. We can use it over and over again every two years. So each time we buy a house and sell it after two years, we can use the exclusion.

While the rules for home sales were radically liberalized in 1997, most people who have been married long enough to have owned more than one home will determine their current home's basis using the old rules. Because varying rules apply depending your given situation, keep in mind that relatively minor changes can significantly affect the tax results of a home sale transaction.

WHEN THE WIFE <u>SHOULD</u> GET THE HOUSE

Despite emotional ties or motivation of payback, there are cases when the wife should keep the house, even when doing so will create an unequal settlement. Keeping in mind equitability vs. equality, let's take a look at the case of Bill and Barbara.

Bill and Barbara are 45 and 49 respectively and were married for 18 years. They have one son, age 16. Bill earns $2,175 per month minus child support payments of $413. His living expenses are $1,400 per month, which leaves him with a surplus of $362 per month. Barbara earns $780 per month plus $413 child support. Her living expenses with the son are $1,630 per month, which creates a *negative* cash flow of $437 per month.

	Barbara	**Bill**
Take-home pay	$ 780	$ 2,175
Living expenses	−$ 1,630	−$ 1,400
Child support	+$ 413	−$ 413
Cash flow	−$ 437	$ 362

The judge decided the following settlement: Barbara would receive the house, which had equity of $44,100 and her IRA worth $5,000. Bill will get his IRA worth $8,900. There are no other assets. Since Barbara got the house with $44,000 worth of equity, she has to pay Bill half of that equity upon the first of the following events: if she sells the house, if she remarries, or upon the emancipation of the child, which varies from state to state. We do not know if she is going to sell the house or remarry, but we do know that the son is going to turn 18 within two years.

Barbara's house payment is $290 per month with 10 years left on the mortgage. According to this scenario, Barbara is heading for poverty from the outset. To be able to pay Bill his half of the equity in the house, she *MUST* sell the house. This will force her to rent at a much higher cost than her house payment of $290 per month. In her area, rental prices start at $400 to $450 per month.

This court order is forcing Barbara into severe poverty. In this case, it seems reasonable that Barbara should have been allowed to keep the house without paying Bill half the equity — an unequal but equitable settlement.

WHEN THE WIFE <u>SHOULD NOT</u> GET THE HOUSE

While the following case study focuses on the division of the house and the situations when the wife should not keep the house, there is much more to be learned. The importance of budgets (and sticking to them), lifestyle adjustments, and parenting styles all come in to play.

In the following example of Bob and Cindy, we examine not only the financial pitfalls that can arise but also the overhaul that we must each go through when adjusting to such a life-altering event as divorce.

BOB AND CINDY CASE STUDY

Cindy was 32 years old and Bob 33 when their marriage of 12 years ended with divorce. They have two children — ages 9 and 5 — who will remain with Cindy. Bob has offered to pay $250 per month per child in child support.

Three years ago, Bob started his own business, placing a value of $240,000 on it. He argues that the business is so new that its value cannot be counted on and, therefore, should not be divided.

Cindy needs three more years of school to finish college. She will then be able to earn about $27,400 with a net take-home of about $21,000 per year working part time because of the children. However, while in school she will not be able to earn an income. Bob has offered to help Cindy through school by paying maintenance of $2,500 per month for the next three years.

Cindy's expenses with the two children currently are $5,417 per month ($65,000 per year). This includes her expenses for school, which average $350 per month. Bob earns $120,000 per year and brings home $85,000 per year. His expenses are $3,500 per month ($42,000 per year).

When Bob and Cindy married 12 years ago, they bought a lovely first home with the anticipation of raising their family there. As their marriage became more troubled and Bob's income escalated, Bob thought that buying a dream home for Cindy would fix things. So they turned their first home into a rental and purchased a more elegant home which now has a fair market value of $420,000. The monthly payments are $2,500 per month (principal, interest, taxes, and insurance). Although, the purchase of her dream home didn't "fix" their martial problems, Cindy wants to remain in the house with the children.

The rental house is now worth $220,000 with a mortgage of $120,000.

Their IRAs total $34,000. They have credit card debt that totals $22,600.

Bob has proposed that Cindy take the house to live in with the children. She should also take the rental and sell it, the IRAs, and the debt. Bob will keep only his business.

SCENARIO #1
BOB'S PROPOSAL

BOB'S AND CINDY'S ASSET LIST

Item		Value	Cindy	Bob
Home				
FMV	$420,000			
Mortgage	$320,000			
Equity	$100,000	$100,000	$100,000	
Rental Property				
FMV	$220,000			
Mortgage	$120,000			
Selling costs	($13,200)			
Equity	$86,800	$86,800	$86,800	
Business		$300,000		$300,000
IRAs		$34,000	$34,000	
Debt		($22,600)	($22,600)	
TOTAL		$498,200	$198,200	$300,000

Bob feels that since his business is so new and cannot be counted on, he is making a very generous proposal if he takes his business and gives Cindy all the other assets, as well as the debt.

As is often the case with all couples, Bob and Cindy had trouble keeping within their budget while they were married. Cindy tended to overspend and thus increased their credit card debt. Bob on the other hand continued to purchase elegant and luxurious items for Cindy in an attempt to "fix" their marriage. The challenge for Cindy in this case will be the re-education of the importance of staying within her budget. Since she has become accustomed to a particular type of lifestyle over the years, it is essential for her to re-evaluate her current situation – including her definition of "affordable."

Here is a summary overview of their martial division in scenario # 1:

Cindy's Financial Sheet			Version # 1										
Year	Age	Net Salary	Support	Child Support	Living Expenses	Mortgage	Expense Adjust	Tax Liabilit	Cash Flow	Liquid Assets	Retirement	Real Estate Equity	Net Worth
Rate/Durati		4.00%	3 years	14 years	4.00%	30 years		15%		5.50%	7.50%	4.0%	
2004	32		$30,000	$10,800	$40,729	$24,271		$4,500		$86,800	$34,000	$100,000	$220,800
2004	32		$30,000	$10,800	$44,594	$24,271	$3,865	$4,500	($32,565)	$59,009	$34,000	$100,000	$193,009
2005	33		$30,000	$10,800	$46,377	$24,271		$4,500	($34,349)	$27,906	$36,550	$120,377	$184,832
2006	34		$30,000	$10,800	$48,232	$24,271		$4,500	($36,204)		$30,274	$141,665	$171,939
2007	35	$21,000		$10,800	$45,962	$24,271	($4,200)		($38,433)	($14,025)		$163,908	$149,883
2008	36	$21,840		$10,800	$47,800	$24,271			($39,432)	($54,228)		$187,150	$132,922
2009	37	$22,714		$10,800	$49,712	$24,271			($40,470)	($97,681)		$211,439	$113,758
2010	38	$23,622		$10,800	$51,701	$24,271			($41,550)	($144,603)		$236,825	$92,222
2011	39	$24,567		$10,800	$53,769	$24,271			($42,673)	($195,229)		$263,359	$68,130
2012	40	$25,550		$10,800	$55,919	$24,271			($43,841)	($249,808)		$291,098	$41,290
2013	41	$26,572		$10,800	$58,156	$24,271			($45,056)	($308,603)		$320,097	$11,494
2014	42	$27,635		$5,400	$55,082	$24,271	($5,400)		($46,319)	($371,896)		$350,419	($21,477)
2015	43	$28,740		$5,400	$57,286	$24,271			($47,417)	($439,767)		$382,126	($57,641)
2016	44	$29,890		$5,400	$59,577	$24,271			($48,559)	($512,514)		$415,287	($97,227)
2017	45	$31,085		$5,400	$61,960	$24,271			($49,747)	($590,449)		$449,970	($140,479)
2018	46	$32,329			$59,039	$24,271	($5,400)		($50,982)	($673,905)		$486,251	($187,654)
2019	47	$33,622			$57,535	$24,271	($3,865)		($48,185)	($759,155)		$524,207	($234,948)
2020	48	$34,967			$59,837	$24,271			($49,142)	($850,050)		$563,920	($286,129)
2021	49	$36,365			$62,230	$24,271			($50,136)	($946,939)		$605,478	($341,461)

Bob's Financial Sheet			Version # 1										
Year	Age	Net Salary	Support	Child Support	Living Expenses	Expense Adjust	Tax Liabilit	Cash Flow	Liquid Asse	Retirement	Business	Net Worth
Rate/Duratid		4.00%	3 years	14 years	4.00%		33%		5.50%	7.50%	4.00%	
2004	33	$85,000	($30,000)	$10,800	$42,000		($9,900)				$300,000	$300,000
2004	33	$85,000	($30,000)	($10,800)	$42,000		($9,900)	$12,100	$12,100		$300,000	$312,100
2005	34	$88,400	($30,000)	($10,800)	$43,680		($9,900)	$13,820	$26,586		$312,000	$338,586
2006	35	$91,936	($30,000)	($10,800)	$45,427		($9,900)	$15,609	$43,657		$324,480	$368,137
2007	36	$95,613		($10,800)	$47,244			$37,569	$83,627		$337,459	$421,086
2008	37	$99,438		($10,800)	$49,134			$39,504	$127,730		$350,958	$478,688
2009	38	$103,415		($10,800)	$51,099			$41,516	$176,271		$364,996	$541,267
2010	39	$107,552		($10,800)	$53,143			$43,609	$229,575		$379,596	$609,171
2011	40	$111,854		($10,800)	$55,269			$45,785	$287,987		$394,780	$682,766
2012	41	$116,328		($10,800)	$57,480			$48,048	$351,874		$410,571	$762,445
2013	42	$120,982		($10,800)	$59,779			$50,402	$421,630		$426,994	$848,624
2014	43	$125,821		($5,400)	$62,170			$58,251	$503,070		$444,073	$947,143
2015	44	$130,854		($5,400)	$64,657			$60,797	$591,535		$461,836	$1,053,372
2016	45	$136,088		($5,400)	$67,243			$63,444	$687,514		$480,310	$1,167,824
2017	46	$141,531		($5,400)	$69,933			$66,198	$791,526		$499,522	$1,291,048
2018	47	$147,192			$72,730			$74,462	$909,522		$519,503	$1,429,025
2019	48	$153,080			$75,640			$77,441	$1,036,986		$540,283	$1,577,269

- Cindy with no income for three years, and then take-home pay of $21,000, increasing at 4% per year.
- Maintenance of $30,000 per year for three years.
- Child support of $10,800 per year for 10 years and then dropping to $5,400 per year until the second child emancipates.
- Cindy's expenses of $65,000 per year, which includes the $2,500 per month mortgage payment. Her expenses increase at 4% per year for inflation.
- Cindy pays off the credit card debt at $322 per month, which takes 15 years.
- Cindy reduces her expenses as each child leaves home.
- Cindy sells the rental property and invests that money at 5% after tax.
- Cindy has the $34,000 in IRAs invested at 7.5%.
- Cindy owns the house with equity of $100,000 equity.
- Bob's take-home pay is $85,000 per year, increasing at 4% per year.
- Bob's expenses are $42,000 per year, increasing at 4% per year for inflation.
- Bob is paying child support and maintenance.
- Bob has no investment assets to start but he invests all excess cash at 5% after-tax.
- Bob's business grows at 4% per year.

The following graph shows the result of scenario # 1:

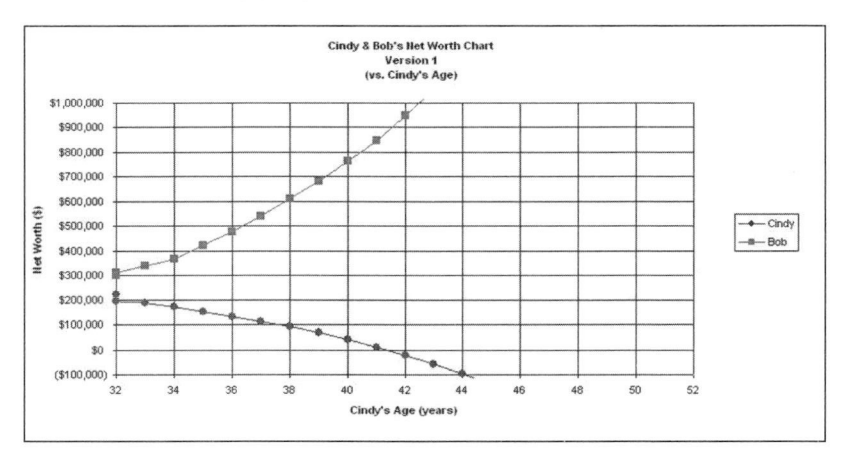

In three years by age 34, Cindy's spendable assets have been depleted; her IRAs are gone by the following year. She does have the house; but she can't use the house to buy groceries.

The result of scenario 1? By keeping her dream house with such a high mortgage payment equal to her alimony payment, Cindy simply can't keep up with her monthly expenses and, in the end, uses up her investments to fund her life style.

SCENARIO # 2
A 50/50 DIVISION

What changes can be made in Scenario #1 to make this a more equitable settlement? The first thing is to look at the 50/50 property division that had been agreed upon. In order to make this a more equitable settlement, one option would be to have Bob pay Cindy a set amount to even up the property division. Since Bob is taking only his business and has no other asset to give to Cindy, a Property Settlement Note is an ideal solution. In this case, Bob would owe Cindy $50,900 to even up the property division. As such, they agreed on a 10-year note at 5% interest which would pay Cindy $550 per month or $6,600 per year. Since this is still a division of the property, it is a non-taxable event except for the interest. In addition, Cindy also negotiated an additional three years of alimony at a reduced amount of $2,000 per month or $24,000 a year.

Cindy's Financial Sheet   Version # 2

Year	Age	Net Salary	Other Income	Support	Child Support	Living Expenses	Mortgage	Expense Adjust	Tax Liabilit	Cash Flow	Liquid Assets	Retirement	Real Estate Equity	Net Worth
Rate/Durati		4.00%		7 years	14 years	4.00%	30 years		15%		5.50%	7.50%	4.0%	
2004	32			$30,000	$10,800	$40,729	$24,271		$4,500		$86,800	$34,000	$100,000	$220,800
2004	32		$6,592	$30,000	$10,800	$44,594	$24,271	$3,865	$4,500	($25,973)	$65,601	$34,000	$100,000	$199,601
2005	33		$6,592	$30,000	$10,800	$46,377	$24,271		$4,500	($27,757)	$41,452	$36,550	$120,377	$198,379
2006	34		$6,592	$30,000	$10,800	$48,232	$24,271		$4,500	($29,612)	$14,120	$39,291	$141,665	$195,077
2007	35	$21,000	$6,592	$24,000	$10,800	$45,962	$24,271	($4,200)	$3,600	($11,441)	$3,456	$42,238	$163,908	$209,602
2008	36	$21,840	$6,592	$24,000	$10,800	$47,800	$24,271		$3,600	($12,440)		$33,681	$187,160	$220,831
2009	37	$22,714	$6,592	$24,000	$10,800	$49,712	$24,271		$3,600	($13,478)		$18,236	$211,439	$229,676
2010	38	$23,622	$6,592	$24,000	$10,800	$51,701	$24,271		$3,600	($14,558)		$194	$236,825	$237,018
2011	39	$24,567	$6,592		$10,800	$53,769	$24,271			($36,081)	($35,925)		$263,359	$227,434
2012	40	$25,550	$6,592		$10,800	$55,919	$24,271			($37,249)	($75,150)		$291,098	$215,948
2013	41	$26,572	$6,592		$10,800	$58,156	$24,271			($38,464)	($117,747)		$320,097	$202,350
2014	42	$27,635			$5,400	$55,082	$24,271	($5,400)		($46,319)	($170,543)		$350,419	$179,876
2015	43	$28,740			$5,400	$57,286	$24,271			($47,417)	($227,340)		$382,126	$154,787
2016	44	$29,890			$5,400	$59,577	$24,271			($48,559)	($288,403)		$415,287	$126,884
2017	45	$31,085			$5,400	$61,960	$24,271			($49,747)	($354,011)		$449,970	$95,959
2018	46	$32,329				$59,039	$24,271	($5,400)		($50,982)	($424,464)		$486,251	$61,787
2019	47	$33,622				$57,535	$24,271	($3,865)		($48,185)	($495,994)		$524,207	$28,213
2020	48	$34,967				$59,837	$24,271			($49,142)	($572,415)		$563,920	($8,495)
2021	49	$36,365				$62,230	$24,271			($50,136)	($654,034)		$605,478	($48,557)
2022	50	$37,820				$64,719	$24,271			($51,171)	($741,177)		$648,969	($92,208)
2023	51	$39,3??				?99	$24,271			($52,247)	($8?1,189)			($139,698)

Bob's Financial Sheet		Version # 2												
Year	Age	Net Salary	Support	Child Support	Living Expenses	Expense Adjust	Tax Liabilit	Property Note	Total Expenses	Cash Flow	Liquid Asse	Retirement	Business	Net Worth
Rate/Duratio		4.00%	7 years	14 years	4.00%		33%				5.50%	7.50%	4.00%	
2004	33	$85,000	($30,000)	$10,800	$42,000		($9,900)						$300,000	$300,000
2004	33	$85,000	($30,000)	($10,800)	$42,000		($9,900)	$6,592	$38,692	$5,508	$5,508		$300,000	$305,508
2005	34	$88,400	($30,000)	($10,800)	$43,680		($9,900)	$6,592	$40,372	$7,228	$13,039		$312,000	$325,039
2006	35	$91,936	($30,000)	($10,800)	$45,427		($9,900)	$6,592	$42,119	$9,017	$22,773		$324,480	$347,253
2007	36	$95,613	($24,000)	($10,800)	$47,244		($7,920)	$6,592	$45,916	$14,897	$38,923		$337,459	$376,382
2008	37	$99,438	($24,000)	($10,800)	$49,134		($7,920)	$6,592	$47,806	$16,832	$57,895		$350,958	$408,853
2009	38	$103,415	($24,000)	($10,800)	$51,099		($7,920)	$6,592	$49,771	$18,844	$79,924		$364,996	$444,919
2010	39	$107,552	($24,000)	($10,800)	$53,143		($7,920)	$6,592	$51,815	$20,937	$105,256		$379,596	$484,852
2011	40	$111,854		($10,800)	$55,269			$6,592	$61,861	$39,193	$150,238		$394,780	$545,018
2012	41	$116,328		($10,800)	$57,480			$6,592	$64,072	$41,456	$199,958		$410,571	$610,528
2013	42	$120,982		($10,800)	$59,779			$6,592	$66,371	$43,810	$254,766		$426,994	$681,759
2014	43	$125,821		($5,400)	$62,170				$62,170	$58,251	$327,028		$444,073	$771,102
2015	44	$130,854		($5,400)	$64,657				$64,657	$60,797	$405,812		$461,836	$867,648
2016	45	$136,088		($5,400)	$67,243				$67,243	$63,444	$491,576		$480,310	$971,885
2017	46	$141,531		($5,400)	$69,933				$69,933	$66,198	$584,810		$499,522	$1,084,332
2018	47	$147,192			$72,730				$72,730	$74,462	$691,437		$519,503	$1,210,940
2019	48	$153,080			$75,640				$75,640	$77,441	$806,907		$540,283	$1,347,190
2020	49	$159,203			$78,665				$78,665	$80,538	$931,825		$561,894	$1,493,719
2021	50	$165,572			$81,812				$81,812	$83,760	$1,066,835		$584,370	$1,651,205
2022	51	$172,194			$85,084				$85,084	$87,110	$1,212,621		$607,745	$1,820,366
2023	52	$179,082			$88,4..				$88,488	$90,595	$1,369,909		$6??,?55	$2,001,964

The following graph shows the result of scenario #2:

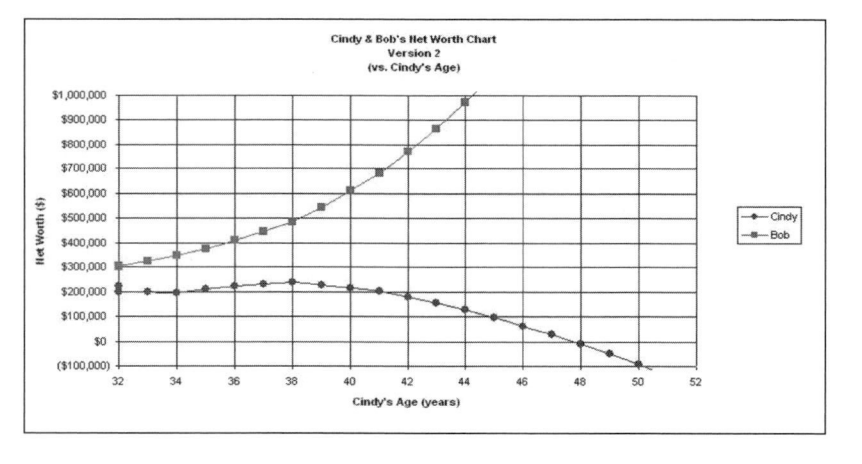

Cindy & Bob's Net Worth Chart
Version 2
(vs. Cindy's Age)

Notice that this additional payout does indeed help Cindy. But remember that this is a Net Worth graph, which includes her house. Her spendable assets are actually gone after the seventh year. It is time for Cindy to think about the wisdom of keeping her dream house and also about her spending habits (the need to curb them that is). It doesn't make economic sense for Cindy to keep a house with a $2,500 per month house payment when she has no income and is relying on alimony to make that payment for her. This is a case that will take a lot of counseling on cash flow and budgeting. Both parties must understand that whatever scenario is followed, it will have a major impact on their financial, emotional, parenting, and relationship lives. Divorce is not easy and requires you to have to make difficult decisions and even accept varying levels of financial freedom in exchange for marital freedom.

SCENARIO #3
A FINAL SOLUTION

- Cindy sells the family home that, after sales costs and paying off the mortgage, gives her $75,000 to invest.
- Cindy does not sell the rental (the first family home) but moves into it. This lowers her mortgage payments and the costs of keeping up the larger house. The net result is a savings of nearly $15,000 per year.
- Cindy asks for $30,000 of alimony per year for six years.
- We show the financial result if Cindy works full time after the first child leaves home.

Cindy's Financial Sheet   Version # 3

Year	Age	Net Salary	Other Income	Support	Child Support	Living Expenses	Mortgage	Expense Adjust	Tax Liabilit	Cash Flow	Liquid Assets	Retirement	Real Estate Equity	Net Worth
Rate/Durati		4.00%		6 years	14 years	4.00%	30 years		15%			5.50%	7.50% 4.0%	
2004	32			$30,000	$10,800	$40,728	$9,102		$4,500		$75,000	$34,000	$100,000	$209,000
2004	32		$6,592	$30,000	$10,800	$44,593	$9,102	$3,865	$4,500	($10,803)	$68,322	$34,000	$100,000	$202,322
2005	33		$6,592	$30,000	$10,800	$46,377	$9,102		$4,500	($12,587)	$59,493	$36,550	$110,141	$206,184
2006	34		$6,592	$30,000	$10,800	$48,232	$9,102		$4,500	($14,442)	$48,323	$39,291	$120,724	$208,339
2007	35	$21,000	$6,592	$30,000	$10,800	$45,961	$9,102	($4,200)	$4,500	$8,829	$59,810	$42,238	$131,769	$233,817
2008	36	$21,840	$6,592	$30,000	$10,800	$47,800	$9,102		$4,500	$7,830	$70,930	$45,406	$143,297	$259,633
2009	37	$22,714	$6,592	$30,000	$10,800	$49,712	$9,102		$4,500	$6,792	$81,623	$48,811	$155,330	$285,765
2010	38	$23,622	$6,592		$10,800	$51,700	$9,102			($19,788)	$66,325	$52,472	$167,892	$286,689
2011	39	$24,567	$6,592		$10,800	$53,768	$9,102			($20,911)	$49,062	$56,408	$181,006	$286,475
2012	40	$25,550	$6,592		$10,800	$55,919	$9,102			($22,079)	$29,681	$60,638	$194,697	$285,016
2013	41	$26,572	$6,592		$10,800	$58,156	$9,102			($23,294)	$8,020	$65,186	$208,993	$282,199
2014	42	$50,000			$5,400	$55,082	$9,102	($5,400)		($8,784)		$69,644	$223,922	$293,567
2015	43	$52,000			$5,400	$57,285	$9,102			($8,987)		$62,885	$239,513	$302,398
2016	44	$54,080			$5,400	$59,577	$9,102			($9,198)		$55,337	$255,797	$311,134
2017	45	$56,243			$5,400	$61,960	$9,102			($9,418)		$46,929	$272,806	$319,735
2018	46	$58,493				$59,038	$9,102	($5,400)		($9,647)		$37,586	$290,574	$328,160
2019	47	$60,833				$57,535	$9,102	($3,865)		($5,804)		$32,667	$309,137	$341,804
2020	48	$63,266				$59,836	$9,102			($5,672)		$27,555	$328,532	$356,086
2021	49	$65,797				$62,229	$9,102			($5,535)		$22,242	$348,798	$371,040
2022	50	$68,428				$64,719	$9,102			($5,392)		$16,721	$369,977	$386,697
2023	51	$7...							$9,102		($5,244)		$10,983		$403,095

Year	Age	Net Salary	Support	Child Support	Living Expenses	Expense Adjust	Tax Liability	Property Note	Total Expenses	Cash Flow	Liquid Assets	Retirement	Business	Net Worth
Rate/Duration		4.00%	6 years	14 years	4.00%		33%				5.50%	7.50%	4.00%	
2004	33	$85,000	($30,000)	$10,800	$42,000	($9,900)							$300,000	$300,000
2004	33	$85,000	($30,000)	($10,800)	$42,000	($9,900)		$6,592	$38,692	$5,508	$5,508		$300,000	$305,508
2005	34	$88,400	($30,000)	($10,800)	$43,680	($9,900)		$6,592	$40,372	$7,228	$13,039		$312,000	$325,039
2006	35	$91,936	($30,000)	($10,800)	$45,427	($9,900)		$6,592	$42,119	$9,017	$22,773		$324,480	$347,253
2007	36	$95,613	($30,000)	($10,800)	$47,244	($9,900)		$6,592	$43,936	$10,877	$34,903		$337,459	$372,362
2008	37	$99,438	($30,000)	($10,800)	$49,134	($9,900)		$6,592	$45,826	$12,812	$49,634		$350,958	$400,592
2009	38	$103,415	($30,000)	($10,800)	$51,099	($9,900)		$6,592	$47,791	$14,824	$67,188		$364,996	$432,184
2010	39	$107,552		($10,800)	$53,143			$6,592	$59,735	$37,017	$107,900		$379,596	$487,496
2011	40	$111,854		($10,800)	$55,269			$6,592	$61,861	$39,193	$153,028		$394,780	$547,807
2012	41	$116,328		($10,800)	$57,480			$6,592	$64,072	$41,456	$202,901		$410,571	$613,471
2013	42	$120,982		($10,800)	$59,779			$6,592	$66,371	$43,810	$257,871		$426,994	$684,864
2014	43	$125,821		($5,400)	$62,170				$62,170	$58,251	$330,304		$444,073	$774,377
2015	44	$130,854		($5,400)	$64,657				$64,657	$60,797	$409,267		$461,836	$871,103
2016	45	$136,088		($5,400)	$67,243				$67,243	$63,444	$495,221		$480,310	$975,531
2017	46	$141,531		($5,400)	$69,933				$69,933	$66,198	$588,657		$499,522	$1,088,179
2018	47	$147,192			$72,730				$72,730	$74,462	$695,495		$519,503	$1,214,998
2019	48	$153,080			$75,640				$75,640	$77,441	$811,188		$540,283	$1,351,471
2020	49	$159,203			$78,665				$78,665	$80,538	$936,341		$561,894	$1,498,236
2021	50	$165,572			$81,812				$81,812	$83,760	$1,071,600		$584,370	$1,655,970
2022	51	$172,194			$85,084				$85,084	$87,110	$1,217,648		$607,745	$1,825,393
2023	52	$179,082			$88,488				$88,488	$90,595	$1,375,213		$632,056	$2,007,268

The result is shown in graph #3:

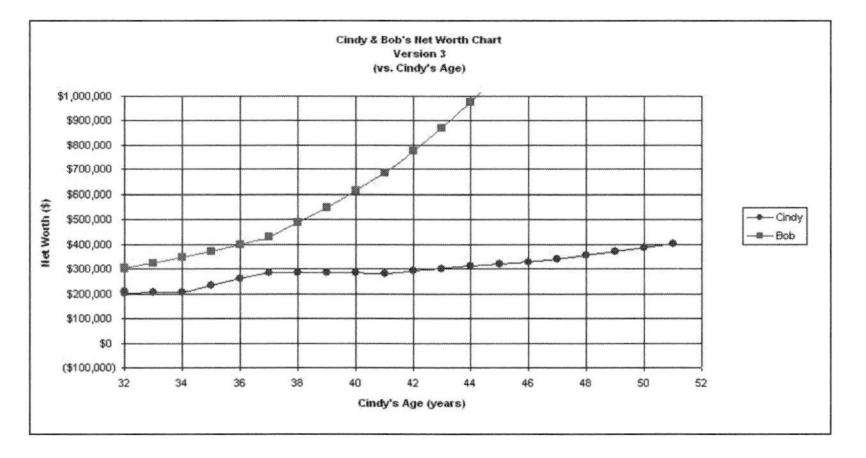

Cindy & Bob's Net Worth Chart
Version 3
(vs. Cindy's Age)

This scenario has helped Cindy the most. It is important for her to realize that her graph will never go up at the same rate as Bob's because he earns much more than she does. A series of charts such as these help couples reach settlements because it gives them better information to make better decisions. In this case, it was important that Cindy see the financial result of her keeping a large house that she couldn't afford.

Summary

- The revised tax laws of 1997 granted each spouse the ability to exclude up to $250,000 if they had lived in the house for two out of the past five years. As such, be sure that the issue of capital gains is addressed in your final settlement.
- Find out the basis in your house before settling! The basis is the amount originally invested in the property minus improvements, sales costs etc.
- Consider the use of a property settlement note. Sometimes there just isn't enough cash or other assets for one spouse to "buy-out" the other. The use of a property settlement note is similar to a bank note in which you determine the number of months, the amount of the payment and so forth.
- Re-evaluate your lifestyle and current spending habits. Divorce often means drastic financial changes. You must be prepared to alter your lifestyle to ensure continued living within your means. You can't assume that your spouse will be as generous as Bob was willing to be with Cindy in the above example.

chapter 4

PENSIONS: HIS, HERS...
OR THEIRS?

Frank and Emily are in the midst of a divorce. Frank has a defined benefit pension which will pay him $2,300 per month upon retirement. Emily decides that a few thousand dollars is not worth fighting over — besides she would rather get the $12,000 baby-grand piano they recently purchased for their den.

Wrong decision. Emily has made a costly mistake. Why? Because the present value of Frank's pension is more than $250,000! Instead of taking the piano, she could have exchanged her half of Frank's pension upfront for $125,000 worth of another asset, leaving Frank with his pension. Or she could have chosen to wait until Frank retires to obtain her share of the martial portion of his benefit. What seemed to have only been a few thousand dollars on the surface, proved to be a costly mistake in the end.

Retirement plans, even though they are in one name only, are marital assets that can be divided at the time of divorce and should not be taken lightly or overlooked. It is important to know the value of each account and to have an awareness of the various rules of liquidating them.

What can seem like an obvious decision, may have long-term consequences in the end. It is important to keep in perspective the ability your decisions have to provide you with a financially sound pay-off both in the short- and long-term. As difficult as it may be to turn your back on the set of china valued at $5,000, imagine turning your back on a future financial reward of $50,000!

From the Business and Professional Women Foundation, "Women and Retirement"[1]

- Men are twice as likely to have a private pension plan as women. In 2000, less than one in five retired women received income from pensions (18%), compared to one in three men (31%).
- Women with pensions receive less than half the amount that men receive. In 2000, the medium benefit amount was $4,200 annually for women, compared to $7,800 for men, representing a retirement wage gap of 53%.

This chapter is not meant to make you an expert on pensions (also referred to as retirement plans), nor will it teach you how to evaluate them. There are volumes written on this subject! Rather, it is to make you aware of their variations and the challenges they present to your fair settlement.

Pensions are recognized as property to be divided upon divorce, provided that all or part is not considered to be separate property. Pensions and retirement benefits that are earned during the marriage are potentially of great value. In fact, if your marriage has been lengthy, it may be your most valuable asset.

There is a bewildering array of basic plans, with countless diverse provisions. However, I will attempt to provide a very general explanation and understanding.

There are two main types of retirement or pension plans: defined contribution and defined benefit. Here's a very basic explanation of the two types and how they work. This information is very important when evaluating your different settlement options. If you need additional information, I would suggest sitting down with a financial advisor or Financial Divorce Specialist before your divorce to discuss your situation.

DEFINED CONTRIBUTION PLAN

In a defined contribution plan, there is very little problem identifying the value of the account. Monthly or quarterly statements will show the dollar amount available to be divided in either the buy–out method or the future share method.

> - Defined contribution plans have cash value today. They issue statements that indicate an actual dollar value of the account.
> - They can be divided equally or un-equally by using a Qualified Domestic Relations Order (QDRO).
> - A portion of a defined contribution plan can be transferred to an IRA for the ex-spouse without tax consequences.
> - Some companies allow a plan account to be divided so that the ex-spouse also has an account with the company.

A common type of defined contribution retirement plan that often comes up in a divorce is the 401(k). But even in the overall group of 401(k)s, there are different types with different rules. Each company can set its own rules for its retirement plans as long as the plan is approved by the IRS.

THREE TYPES OF DEFINED CONTRIBUTION PLANS

Let's say there are three employees. At the end of three years, each employee is in the process of getting a divorce.

Employee A works for a company that has a defined contribution plan. He puts all of his retirement money into the plan and the company does not match any of his funds. He has worked there for three years and he has accumulated $1,500 in his plan. Any money that an employee puts into a 401(k) is the employee's — he or she is 100 percent vested. If he quits or is fired, he can take all of this money with him. He can use it as income, declaring such to the IRS (and most likely, receiving a penalty of 10 percent of the withdrawn amount) or he can roll it over to an IRA.

	Employee A
Length of employment	3 years
Plan value at time of divorce	$1,500
Percent vested	100%
Marital portion	$1,500

Employee B works for a company where only the employer contributes money to the defined contribution plan. The employee does not put anything in. He has worked there for three years and his plan is worth $1,500. The company uses a vesting schedule, which regulates how much money he can take with him if he quits or if he is fired. The amount depends on how long he has worked for the company. Employee B is 30 percent vested. Therefore, his 401(k) today is worth 30 percent of $1,500 or $450. The lower amount, $450, is assigned to the marital pot of assets.

	Employee A	Employee B
Length of employment	3 years	3 years
Plan value at time of divorce	$1,500	$1,500
Percent vested	100%	30%
Marital portion	$1,500	$450

Employee C works for a company whose policy is that for every dollar he puts into his defined contribution plan, it is matched with 50 cents. He has worked there for three years and he has $1,500 in his plan. Out of $1,500, he has put in $1,000 and the company has put in $500 with its matching program. He is 30 percent vested. However, the $1,000 that he put in was his money, so he is 100% vested in that amount and he can take that whole $1,000. He can take 30 percent of the $500 or $150. Employee C's marital portion of this plan is worth $1,150.

	Employee A	Employee B	Employee C
Employee/Employer contribution			$1/50 cents
Length of employment	3 years	3 years	3 years
Plan value at time of divorce	$1,500	$1,500	$1,500
Percent vested	100%	30%	30%
Marital portion	$1,500	$450	$1,150

The above examples illustrate three different types of vesting in defined contribution plans, depending on a company's policy.

TRANSFERRING ASSETS FROM A DEFINED CONTRIBUTION PLAN

Normally, distributions made before the participant reaches age 59-½ are called "early distributions," and are subject to a 10% penalty tax. The tax does not apply to early distributions upon death, disability, annuity payments for the life expectancy of the individual, or distributions made to an ex-spouse by a QDRO.

> **Tax Reg (72)(t)(2)(C) states that when you take money out of a qualified plan in accordance with a written divorce instrument (a QDRO), the recipient can spend any or all of it without paying the 10% penalty.**

Let's take a look at what happens when the ex-spouse receives the 401(k) asset. There are some specific rules to be aware of. Here's an example.

Esther was married to an airline pilot who was nearing retirement. They were both age 55. There was $640,000 in his 401(k) and the retirement plan was prepared to transfer $320,000 to her IRA. She could transfer the money to an IRA and pay no taxes on this amount until she withdraws funds from the IRA. But Esther's attorney's fees were $60,000 and she needed another $20,000 to fix her roof. She said, "I need $80,000." She held back $80,000 of the money before transferring the remaining amount into her IRA. She was able to spend the $80,000 without incurring a 10% penalty.

Because the 401(k) withholds 20 percent to apply towards taxes on a withdrawal, Esther should have asked for $100,000. After the 20 percent withholding, she would have $80,000 in cash and $220,000 to transfer to her IRA.

Esther does have to pay the taxes on the entire amount because she had to declare the $80,000 as income but she did not have to pay the 10% early withdrawal penalty.

After the money from a pension plan goes into an IRA, which is *not* considered a qualified plan, Esther is held to the early withdrawal rule. If she says, "Oh I forgot, I need another $5,000 to buy a car," it is too late. She will have to pay the 10% penalty *and* the taxes on that money.

Normally, distributions made before the participant attains age 59-½ are called *early distributions*, and are subject to a 10 percent penalty tax. The tax does not apply to early distributions upon death, disability, annuity payments for the life expectancy of the individual, or distributions made to an ex-spouse by a QDRO.

Tax Code section (72)(t)(2)(C) states that when you take money out of a *qualified* plan in accordance with a written divorce instrument (a QDRO), the recipient can spend any or all of it without paying the 10 percent penalty.

It is important to understand the difference between *rolling over* money from a qualified plan and *transferring money* from a qualified plan. The Unemployment Compensation Amendment Act (UCA), which took effect in January 1993, stated that any money taken out of a qualified plan or tax-sheltered annuity would be subject to 20 percent withholding. This rule does not apply to IRAs.

In other words, if money is *transferred* from a qualified plan to an IRA, the check is sent directly from the qualified plan to the IRA. In a *rollover*, the funds are paid to the person who then remits the money to an IRA. A payment to the person, whether or not there is a rollover, is subject to the 20% withholding. Only a direct transfer avoids the withholding tax.

For example, Henry was to receive his ex-wife Ginny's 401(k) of $100,000, which was invested in the ABC Mutual Fund. He asked the ABC Fund to send him the money so he could rollover the money into a different mutual fund of his choice. The ABC Fund sent Henry $80,000, which was the amount remaining after they withheld the 20% withholding tax.

Henry deposited the $80,000 in his new IRA mutual fund. He could have added the $20,000 which was withheld for taxes, but he didn't have $20,000 to spare even though the IRS would have refunded that amount to him after filing his taxes.

Since he could not come up with the $20,000, the next April when he filed his tax return, he paid an extra $6,600 in state and federal taxes. Of course, when he eventually takes his IRA money, $20,000 in taxes will already have been paid.

If Henry had instead *transferred* the $100,000 from the ABC Mutual Fund to his new fund, he would have $100,000 in his new fund (instead of $80,000) and would have saved $6,600 in taxes. It is important to remember the effect of having an extra $20,000 growing tax-deferred.

> ## IRA transfers must be made directly between trustees and not by a rollover.

IRAs

An IRA is not considered to be a qualified plan, and a rollover may take place without the 20 percent withholding for taxes. In a divorce situation, IRAs may be transferred in whole or in part. Since an IRA is not a qualified plan, a QDRO is not needed to transfer or divide it.

DEFINED BENEFIT PLANS

The courts are struggling with the challenge of how to value and divide pensions. For some cases, they must value the interest in a retirement plan. This interest will not include any portion acquired either after the divorce or, in most states, before the marriage.

There are three different methods used to divide pension benefits:

1. The first is the "present value" or "cash-out" method, which awards the non-employee spouse a lump sum settlement — or a marital asset of equal value — at the time of divorce in return for the employee's keeping the pension.

2. The second method is the "deferred division" or "future share" method where no present value is determined. Each spouse is awarded a share of the benefits if and when they are paid.

3. The third method is the "reserved jurisdiction," whereby the court retains the authority to order distributions from a pension plan at some point in the future. It should be considered a last resort, as it leaves both spouses in limbo with regard to planning for their future.

In many pensions, there are choices as to how it is to be paid out such as life, years certain, life of employee and spouse. The value of a defined benefit plan comes from the company's guarantee to pay based on a predetermined plan formula, not from an account balance.

For instance, the amount of monthly pension could be determined by a complex calculation which could include, in addition to the employee's final average salary, an annuity factor based on the employee's age at retirement, the employee's annual average Social Security tax base, the employee's total number of years of employment and age at retirement, the method chosen by the employee to receive payment of voluntary and required contributions, and whether a pension will be paid to a survivor upon the employee's death. As you might guess, the valuation of such a plan poses a challenge and has fostered much creativity!

TRANSFERRING ASSETS FROM A DEFINED BENEFIT PLAN

Here's an example of how a defined benefit plan works with Henry and Ginny from the previous example. Assume that based on today's earnings and his length of time with the company, Henry will receive $1,200 a month at age 65 from his pension. He is now age 56, and has to wait nine more years before he can start receiving the $1,200 per month. Because of the wait, it is called a *future benefit*. You can though value this future stream of income and calculate a present value of what it is worth today. This present value can be used in the list of assets for purposes of dividing property.

You could, for example, divide the defined benefit plan according to a QDRO by saying that Ginny will receive $600 when Henry retires. However, when he retires, his benefit will probably be worth more than $1,200 per month because he will have worked there longer. When Henry retires, he may get $1,800 a month, but if the QDRO stated that Ginny would receive $600 per month, she won't get any more even though the value of the fund has increased.

It is important to find out whether (1) the $1,200 per month is what he will get at age 65 based on today's earnings and time with the company, or (2) the $1,200 per month assumes it is what he will get if he stays with he company until age 65 with projected earnings built in. If it is not clear on the pension statements, these questions must be asked of the plan administrator.

If the couple has less than eight years to wait until retirement, Ginny may choose to wait to get the $600 per month so she can have guaranteed income. However, if they are 9, 10, or more years away from retirement, she may wish to trade out another asset up front. This way, she'll be assured of getting some funding.

QUALIFIED DOMESTIC RELATIONS ORDER (QDRO)

The QDRO is an order from the court to the retirement plan administrator, spelling out how the plan's benefits are to be assigned to each party in a divorce. It is a legal document, creating both problems and liabilities with it. QDROs must be done by professionals who know what they are doing — an attorney or someone who specializes in QDROs.

Plans divisible by a QDRO include defined contribution plans and defined benefit plans, 401(k)s, thrift savings plans, some profit-sharing and money-purchase plans, Keogh plans, tax sheltered annuities, Employee Stock Ownership Plans (ESOPs), and the old Payroll Based Employee Stock Ownership Plan (PAYSOPs).

Plans that are not divisible by a QDRO include some plans of small employers not covered by ERISA and many public employee group funds such as police and fire groups, and city, state, and other governmental employees including federal employees.

The QDRO is sent to the employer's pension plan administrator. It tells how much of the money in the plan is to be sent to the spouse of the employee. This amount can be from zero to 100 percent, depending on how they have divided the other assets. It does not automatically mean 50 percent. Typically, the QDRO tells not only how the money in the plan is to be divided, but what is to happen when the parties die.

LIMITATIONS IN USING A QDRO

The pension documents should be looked at during the divorce proceedings and before the divorce is final. There are too many horror stories where a case has gone to court, everything is settled, the QDRO has been presented to the judge, and the judge says the divorce is final. Then, the QDRO is sent to the pension plan and the ex-spouse ends up not getting any money. Why? Because the plan (doesn't have to and) won't pay it.

A QDRO generally may not require that the plan provides any form of benefit not otherwise offered under the plan, and may not require that the plan provides increased benefits either. However, within certain limits, it is permissible for a QDRO to require that payments to the alternate payee begin on or after the participant's earliest retirement age, even though the participant has not retired at that time. One area of liability in drafting a QDRO for a pension plan is when the pension documents do not allow for the ex-spouse to receive benefits before the employee spouse has retired.

PUBLIC EMPLOYEES PENSIONS

Another type of defined benefit plan is for public employees such as schoolteachers, principals, librarians, firemen, policemen, and state troopers. This type of plan typically will not allow any division by order of a QDRO in a divorce and in some states is not assignable at all to the ex-spouse.

Each year, the employee gets a statement showing his or her contributions to this plan. This sum of money (plus interest) is what the employee can take if he quits or is fired. However, if the employee stays in the job for a minimum number of years (usually 20 or 25), he or she will receive an annuity retirement payout that is a percent of their final average pay. It is at retirement time that the employee sees the contribution of the public employer.

Janice and Frank had been married for 23 years. Frank started out as a schoolteacher. At the time of their divorce, he was the Principal of the high school in their small city. The statement of his retirement account showed that he had paid in $82,050 and that is the number that Frank used as his value of his retirement. His attorney accepted this number.

Janice's attorney encouraged her to hire a Financial Divorce Specialist who determined that, when Frank retires, he would get 60 percent of his final average salary, or $32,050 per year. The financial expert testified in court that the Present Value of the marital portion of that future stream of income was $373,060 — a far cry from $82,050! The judge, after dividing all the other assets equally, declared that Frank still owed Janice $133,585 which should be paid to her via a property settlement note over 20 years at $957 per month.

SURVIVOR BENEFITS

Keep in mind when the defined benefit plan is divided, it is critical to work with the plan administrator in setting up survivor benefits. An ex-wife, for example, would be unhappy if she got 50 percent of the defined benefit plan and then the ex-husband died and the rest of the money wasn't paid out. The QDRO needs to state it simplistically — joint and survivor annuity — which, of course, will have a reduction in ultimate benefit — the 40 percent or whatever — and have it set up in a separate account. It will all be calculated and annualized at the time of payment.

For example, an ex-wife can preserve her right to receive survivor's benefits if her husband should die before retirement. This means that, before he can waive such coverage, an ex-husband must obtain his ex-wife's written consent and have it notarized, *even if he has remarried and wants his new spouse to receive the benefits instead.* A divorce decree that earmarks the money for a former spouse can override the rights of a second or third spouse.

VESTING

Vesting refers to the employee's entitlement to retirement benefits. A participant is vested when he or she has an immediate, fixed right of present or future enjoyment of the accrued benefit. The percentage of vesting means what the employee is entitled to the retirement plan when he or she retires, quits, or is fired.

When *fully vested,* an employee is entitled to all the benefits that the employer has contributed. Being *partially vested* means that if the employee quit the job, he or she would be able to take that percentage of the employer's contributions. An example would be if the employee were 30 percent vested and the employer's contributions were $1,500, the employee could take $450.

Any contributions made by the employee to the plan are immediately 100 percent vested. The employee is always entitled to take all of his contributions plus the earnings on those contributions.

It is important at divorce to find out whether the state considers non-vested retirement benefits to be marital property. If so, a defined contribution plan's total value could be divided, and the employee could leave his job and never receive the nonvested amounts.

For example, Marvin worked for ABC, Inc. His 401(k) was worth $58,000, which was made up of $12,300 from his contributions and $45,700 from his employer's contributions. Marvin is 40 percent vested. If he quit his job today, he could take his own $12,300 and $18,280 of his employer's contributions for a total of $30,580. He and his ex-wife Susie agreed to value his 401(k) at the full $58,000 for purposes of dividing property. Marvin kept his 401(k) and paid Susie $29,000 for her half out of the savings account money. Six months after the divorce was final, ABC, Inc. laid off half its workforce including Marvin. He left the company with $30,580 from his retirement account. The net result was that he ended up $13,710 short in the division of marital property.

MATURE PLANS

An employee may be fully vested but may still have to wait until he or she reaches a certain age before being able to receive any benefits. For instance, some companies do not pay out benefits until the employee has reached age 60 or age 65.

And in some cases, if the employee is not vested in the plan and dies before retirement age, the benefits are lost. Nobody gets them.

DOUBLE DIPPING

Sometimes a retirement plan is divided at divorce as part of the property division. Then in some states, when the employee retires, his income from his portion of the retirement plan is considered when calculating alimony and/or child support. The end result is that the non-employee spouse is getting paid twice from the same asset. What is used as income in determining alimony depends on state law.

THE CARROT STORY

Understanding how defined benefit pensions really work is often confusing to even the most knowledgeable individual or even professional for that matter. The following excerpt from *Assigning Retirement Benefits In Divorce* by Gale S. Finley is an excellent and delightful way to learn and comprehend the ins and outs of defined benefit plans.[2]

Imagine a farm in central Kentucky that raises racehorses. The owner of the farm takes his racing very seriously and comes up with a way to reward his horses for winning races for him. He calls it the "Carrot Retirement Plan." He decides that after each horse retires from racing, it will be provided an allocation of carrots each week as a supplement to its regular diet. The number of carrots a horse receives each week depends upon the number of races it wins during its racing career. Each horse will receive its weekly allotment of carrots until it goes to that big pasture in the sky.

In order to ensure an adequate supply of carrots for his retiring horses, the owner decides to plan ahead and start growing and freezing carrots. He sits down with the veterinarian and the two of them decide how many carrots he will have to grow and store each week. They look at how many horses he has, how many races each has won, when each is expected to retire, and how long each is expected to live after retirement. Based upon those initial projections, the owner comes up with a quantity of carrots that will be needed to be planted that first year. He hires an expert in carrot growing — the Keeper of the Carrots — to maintain a carrot crop that will continue to produce an adequate supply to meet future carrot obligations.

The next year, the owner again sits down with his veterinarian and the Keeper of the Carrots. The owner and the veterinarian discuss factors bearing on the number of carrots that will be needed for all the retiring horses down the road, such as any new horses acquired during the year, any that have died during the year, how many races each has won, and how many will be retiring. Also, they reevaluate their projections from the previous year concerning all those same factors based upon what actually occurred during the year. The Keeper of the Carrots then reports on how well the carrot crop came in during the year and whether it will be adequate given the number of carrots the owner has projected under the Carrot Retirement Plan. They also discuss the number of carrots that will have to be planted during the next year.

Each year these three people sit down and look at the events that have occurred during the year and how those events affect future carrot obligations. The goal is always for the three of them to work together to ensure that, at retirement, each horse is given its proper weekly allotment of carrots for as long as it lives. If during a given year fewer horses than were projected are retiring, more retiring horses died than were expected to, some horses died while still active, and/or the Keeper of the Carrots brought in a bumper crop, fewer, if any, new carrots have to be planted. On the other hand, negative results as compared to the projections mean more carrots than expected must be planted.

Let's look at one of the horses covered under the Carrot Retirement Plan (the "Participant Horse"). This Participant Horse is still actively racing and occasionally winning. In addition, he has won enough races through today's date to be entitled to receive 10 carrots each week of his life beginning on the date he is permanently turned out to pasture (its "Accrued Carrot Benefit"). What can we say about this horse's rights under the Carrot Retirement Plan as of today's date? What the Participant Horse has today is a right to receive 10 carrots each week for life beginning at some future date. If he wins more races in the future, the number of weekly carrots to which he is entitled will increase. But as of today, 10 per week is the number. Remember though, it is a current right to receive carrots in the future if the Participant Horse lives long enough to receive them. The Participant Horse does not "own" any carrots. Because he is still racing, he is not currently entitled to any carrots. In fact, because he may die before he retires, he may never be entitled to receive any carrots. The owner of the horse farm owns thousands of carrots that are being stored to someday give the Participant Horse and all his co-retirees a certain number of carrots each week for their respective lives. But the Participant Horse does not own any carrots until he actually receives his first weekly allotment.

Assuming another horse — the "A-P Horse" — wants to lay claim to 50% of the Participant Horse's Accrued Carrot Benefit, what do we have to divide? We have the Participant Horse's right to receive 10 carrots per week for his life beginning when he retires. We can split that down the middle so that the A-P Horse will get 5 carrots from each 10 carrot allotment as it is distributed to the Participant Horse during his lifetime. That is the easiest way to make the division because the number of carrots to be given, the beginning date, and the ending date are already determined. No muss and no fuss.

As simple as that method may be, however, it means that the A-P Horse has absolutely no control over any aspect of the carrot distribution process. The A-P Horse may want to start receiving her carrots sooner or later than the Participant Horse's retirement date. The A-P Horse may want the security of knowing the carrots will keep coming during her lifetime rather than the lifetime of the Participant Horse (rumor has it the Participant Horse's health is deteriorating). Can we simply provide that the A-P Horse will receive 5 carrots each week during her life, beginning when she chooses? We can't if our goal is to give the A-P Horse a right to only 50% of the Participant Horse's Accrued Carrot Benefit as of today's date.

To understand that, let's look at what the Participant Horse's Accrued Carrot Benefit roughly translates to. We will assume that the Participant Horse will be retired in 2 years and will start receiving 10 carrots each week, beginning November 1 of that year. At that time the Participant Horse will have a life expectancy of 20 years. If these assumptions hold true, the owner will need to be prepared to provide 10,400 carrots (10 carrots × 52 weeks × 20 years) to the Participant Horse over his lifetime. If we assume a 50/50 split of the amount so that the Participant Horse receives only 5 carrots per week, the lifetime total becomes 5,200 carrots.

Now, let's assume the A-P Horse, because of an age difference, has a current life expectancy of 24 years. If the A-P Horse starts to receive 5 carrots per week (based upon the 50% assignment) starting now (assuming this is the "earliest retirement age") and continuing for the assumed 24 years, she will receive an aggregate of 6,240 carrots over her lifetime. This is substantially more than the 5,200 that represent 50% of the Accrued Carrot Benefit. Moreover, when added to the 5,200 the owner expects to give to the Participant Horse, the total (11,440) is significantly higher than the 10,400 that would be given (if all assumptions are accurate) to the Participant Horse if no assignment is made. Since a predicted 10,400 is all the owner is obligated for under the Carrot Retirement Plan, something has to give.

If, in fact, the intent of the parties is to give the A-P Horse during her lifetime the equivalent of 5,200 carrots over the lifetime of the Participant Horse, a couple of options exist. As we mentioned earlier, the A-P Horse can receive half of the Participant Horse's weekly allotment of carrots while the Participant horse is alive. But to keep carrots coming to the A-P Horse after the Participant Horse dies, she can also require the Carrot Retirement Plan to continue to deliver to her the same weekly allotment. Of course, in order to "fund" her continuing carrot supply after the death of the Participant Horse, the Carrot Retirement Plan will need to reduce the number of weekly carrots that are given out while the Participant Horse is alive. It would be incorrect to give out 10 carrots per week, 5 to the Participant Horse and 5 to the A-P Horse, who is expected to live longer than the Participant Horse, upon the death of the Participant Horse (assuming she fulfills her life expectancy). Another option is for the A-P Horse to be treated as though she has her own Accrued Carrot Benefit and to receive some smaller number per week beginning when she chooses and continuing for as long as she lives. In our example, the latter option would result in the A-P Horse immediately beginning to receive 4,167 (5200 divided by 24 years divided by 52 weeks) per week for her lifetime.

Either of these 2 options provides the A-P Horse the equivalent of 50% of the participant Horse's Accrued Carrot Benefit because it ends up, if all life expectancy assumptions for the Participant Horse and the A-P Horse hold true, to be the same aggregate number of carrots the Participant Horse will receive during his life.[2]

Summary

- Get your pension appraised! As I've illustrated in this chapter, not getting your spouse's pension appraised could be the difference between splitting $80,000 or $350,000! Although these plans can be complicated to value, as we've seen, they can be worth a significant amount of money.
- Use a QDRO! A Qualified Domenstic Relations Order is a legal document used to tell the administrator how much money from the retirement plan to send to the ex-spouse. Remember: It is the only way for the ex-spouse to get payout from a qualified plan such as a 401(k).
- Save yourself money — don't pay the 10% penalty! There are ways to avoid having to pay the 10% penalty when you have to withdraw cash from a qualified retirement plan such as a 410(k) before you turn 59 ½. Be sure to consult with a professional to help you navigate the tax rules and regulations to avoid any unnecessary penalties.

Notes

1. From the Business and Professional Women Foundation, "Women and Retirement."
2. *Assigning Retirement Benefits in Divorce, A Practical Guide to Negotiating and Drafting QDROs*, by Gale S. Finley, pages 17–21, American Bar Association, 1995.

PART 3

MAKING THEM PAY

chapter 5

ALIMONY

Lucy, age 53, had never worked outside the home. She had agreed to accept three years of "rehabilitative maintenance" after thirty years of marriage. Having spent the last two years training at a local vocational school, she went out to look for work in her new field. No job experience. Fifty-five years old. The market just wasn't interested in her.

Sounds familiar? Or perhaps you have experience but have been raising a family for the last 10 years and too much has changed in your field. What options do you have? What options *did* you have?

Simply put, alimony is a series of payments from one spouse to the other, or to a third party on behalf of the receiving spouse (for all practical purposes, alimony and maintenance mean the same thing). In most cases, the wife is the recipient; in some, the husband receives it. Alimony is taxable income to the person who receives it and tax-deductible by the person who pays it. Calculating alimony comes after the property is divided. The reason for this is that alimony can be based on the amount of property received, so it is important to look first at the property division.

Alimony can be very important for the non-working spouse. Sometimes in a long-term marriage (more than 10 years), either the wife has not worked outside the home or she has stayed home with the children until they are in school or left home. Both of these positions limit her ability to build a career. She and her husband may have decided as a couple that she would be responsible for running the household and/or caring for the children.

In most cases, if she did hold a job, her income was usually less than her husband's — sometimes, substantially lower. If a transfer or move were indicated, the decision would be based on his job and career. If they moved, she would usually have to quit her job and start over somewhere else.

Career decisions and divorce can negatively affect the husband as well. If the wife's career is more lucrative, the husband may have refused a job transfer so that his wife could pursue her career. He is stuck in a dead-end position that he can't leave without jeopardizing his pension.

> When you are "fired" from the job of husband or wife, no one offers you an unemployment check. Is it any wonder then that alimony often becomes a major battleground in divorce?

CRITERIA FOR RECEIVING ALIMONY

It used to be that "fault" determined alimony. Today, while fault may still be a factor in some states, alimony is based on many criteria. Among the most typical are:

- Need
- Ability to pay
- Length of marriage
- Previous lifestyle
- Age and health of both parties

Let's take a look at each factor a bit more closely:

1. Need

"Does the recipient have enough money to live on?" This would include income from earning ability, earnings from property received in the property division, and earnings from separate property. Alimony may be necessary to prevent you or your spouse from becoming dependent upon welfare.

Minor children are also considered when evaluating need. Although child support is a separate issue, the mother (if she is the custodial parent) must be able to care adequately for the children. That means being able to provide a roof over the kid's head, utilities to heat, light and water in their home.

Even though you (or your spouse) may think an alimony award is needed, the court sometimes thinks otherwise. For example: Sophia wanted maintenance from her husband. However, she had a trust set aside that was separate property, and in that trust was over $1 million dollars. The court deemed that she did not need maintenance since she had property that would provide an income to her.

An interesting survey was conducted a few years ago. Judges at a conference were given a divorce case study to gauge what variability there would be in their opinions. The case involved a short-term marriage between two lawyers, in which the wife had developed multiple sclerosis and was in serious condition. The judge's opinions ranged from "No maintenance as it was a short-term marriage" to "Lifetime maintenance because of her health situation" and all points in between.

Looking at the following formula, we can see that there are many problems with relying on it.

$$\frac{\text{Husband's income} - \text{expenses}}{\text{Ability to pay}} \qquad \frac{\text{Wife's expenses} - \text{income}}{\text{Need}}$$

It is easy to say that somewhere in-between his ability to pay and her need is the amount of maintenance to be paid, but questions arise about their true incomes and expenses. It's not as easy as it seems.

2. Ability to Pay

The criterion of ability to pay considers whether the payor can afford to pay what is needed and still have enough to live on or to support a lifestyle roughly equivalent to his or her previous lifestyle.

An angry wife may say, "I want $6,000 a month," which may be the husband's entire salary. The wife is acting on pure emotions. She may be feeling hurt, bitter, angry, and sad at what has become of their marriage.

And what about all the cases where we see his commissions and bonuses dry up when it is time to get divorced? We know that divorce causes an extreme amount of stress and distraction, which greatly impacts his income earning potential. However, we typically see his income go back up after the divorce is final and he once again refocuses on his career. In this situation, income may be imputed to the husband's earning potential when calculating the amount of alimony to be paid.

For instance, there was a famous divorce case out in Boulder, Colorado in which the husband, who had been earning a substantial income, decided to quit his job and go into the mountains to grow mushrooms. The husband claimed he no longer had the income to pay such a high alimony. The judge ruled that since the husband had the income producing *capacity* he could grow mushrooms all he pleased but he would have to figure out how to pay the maintenance that the court awarded the wife.

3. Length of Marriage

The length of your marriage greatly weighs in on the courts decision to not only award alimony but often times the length of that alimony as well. For example, a two-year marriage may not qualify for permanent alimony but a 25-year marriage probably would. However, this still depends on all of the economic factors in the divorce and the property division.

A rule of thumb that is often used is that alimony may be awarded for half the number of years married. However this rule of thumb can be far from the right answer depending on other factors.

Some rules to remember about duration:

- Alimony stops upon the death of either party.
- Alimony usually ends upon the remarriage of the recipient.
- Alimony continues until it is modified (unless the amount and/or duration is non-modifiable).

4. Previous Lifestyle

Previous lifestyle is a criterion that takes into account how each spouse is accustomed to living. In a 23-year marriage where the husband earns over $500,000 per year, he probably won't be able to justify that his wife only needs $50,000 per year in alimony. In contrast, neither member of a young couple who didn't earn much money should not expect to become wealthy as a result of the divorce.

5. Age and Health of Both Parties

The age and health of both parties is the final criteria when deciding alimony. Questions that the judge will ponder include:

- Is he or she disabled?
- Is he already retired? If so, does he have guaranteed permanent income?

- If she is 50 years old and has never worked, it will be very difficult for her to find employment. She may need open-ended
  maintenance.
- If she is in poor mental and/or physical health, she may not be
  able to find adequate employment.

REHABILITATIVE MAINTENANCE

In the 1970s, courts began to recognize the need for a transition
period. It was unrealistic to expect or assume that the wife (or husband
when the wife was the breadwinner) could instantly earn what her
husband did, if ever. With that awakening, rehabilitative maintenance
was born.

If the wife, for example, needs three years of school to finish her
degree or time to update old skills, she may get *rehabilitative maintenance*. This will give her the temporary financial help in the interim
that she needs until she is able to earn an enough to be self-sufficient.

In discussing rehabilitative maintenance, it's important to be realis-
tic. Why? Sometimes a normal three-year degree becomes impossible
while caring for three kids. Realistically, five years may be more in line.
It shouldn't be viewed as an entitlement — to be stretched until every
drop is taken. Rather, a bridge from one "career" to the next.

Finally, depending on all other factors, particularly her age and the
duration of the marriage, paying alimony just for a rehabilitative period
may not be the right result.

MODIFICATION OF MAINTENANCE

The one constant in life is change. Given that, it doesn't make much
sense to assume that the final alimony settlement decided in court will
apply to all future scenarios. Property is almost always final. Alimony is
usually modifiable. For example, one spouse may become unemployed;
the other may become ill. Or the change could be positive. You or your
ex-spouse may land a job that creates lucrative stock options and
incentives; or perhaps you inherited a substantial sum of money, win a
lawsuit or even win the lottery. This type of windfall could lead to a
decrease in maintenance.

To allow some flexibility to accommodate these potential changes, the court where the divorce is granted often maintains "jurisdiction" over the case. This allows any order of support to be modified when a change of circumstances, such as an increase or decrease in income, makes it reasonable to do so.

What if you get a roommate who pays all the expenses? Your ex-spouse's attorney could use this as a fact to reduce the current alimony payment. Some states presume that when a spouse who receives maintenance moves in with another person, he or she needs less monetary support.

After the divorce is final and a modifiable order of support is entered, either your or your spouse can go back into court and ask for a modification (increase or decrease). However, you need to be aware that the judge may deny the request for modification. Not only that, but he or she may even rule in the opposite direction! So, before you go back to court to ask for a modification, be sure to examine your position and the soundness of your evidence with your attorney.

Non-modifiable maintenance is not used very often because it is a challenge to both sides but there are certain advantages to it in limited cases. Let's say that the divorce decree says that he is going to pay six years of maintenance non-modifiable. This means that even if she gets married in two years (provided that the order says the obligation survives remarriage), she still gets four more years of maintenance. While this appears to be a great deal for the recipient, it can work against her. What if she doesn't remarry and instead becomes disabled or otherwise needs more income? She cannot get more. At six years, all payments stop. Legally, she has no way to continue the maintenance income.

Many times, after maintenance is set up, the husband retires early. He won't want to pay maintenance anymore. To change the original orders, he'll have to go back to court and have them changed by a new court order. Even if you both agree, you will have to draw up a new agreement. This means money is spent — you both will have to hire attorneys to get it changed.

Sometimes the parties can't settle and the case will end up in court. Rarely does the wife want to reduce the maintenance amount. Or perhaps he wants to drop it totally, while she is receptive to some decrease, but not a decrease to zero. If they cannot agree on what number should be used, they end up in front of a judge.

For the above reasons, many payers of maintenance prefer the term to be non-modifiable. They know there will be a predetermined end to the stream of payments. It makes it easier for them to accept than to worry about the uncertainty of when closure will take place.

TAX ISSUES OF ALIMONY

To be considered alimony for tax purposes, the payments must meet all of the following requirements:

1. All payments must be made in cash, check or money order.
2. There must be a written court order or separation agreement.
3. The couple may not agree that the payments are not to receive alimony tax treatment.
4. They may not be residing in the same household.
5. The payments must terminate upon the payor's death.
6. They may not file a joint tax return.
7. No portion may be considered child support.

Let's look at each requirement in more detail:

1. **In order to qualify as alimony, payments made from one spouse to the other must be made in cash or the equivalent of cash. Transfers of services or property do not qualify as alimony.**

   a. It is possible for payments made to a third party on behalf of his or her spouse to qualify as alimony.

   Under the terms of their divorce decree, Stanley is required to pay his ex-wife, Marilyn, $5,000 per year for the next five years. Six months after the decree is entered, Marilyn decides to return to school to qualify for a better paying job. She calls Stanley and asks him to pay her $5,000 tuition instead of sending her the monthly alimony checks. Stanley agrees and on September 4, 2003, pays $2,500 for Marilyn's first semester tuition. For Stanley to deduct this payment as alimony, he must obtain a written statement from Marilyn indicating that they agreed that his payment of the tuition was alimony. This written statement must be received before Stanley files his original (not an amended) income tax return for 2003.

As tax return time approaches, Stanley is eager to get his tax refund. On February 14, 2004 he files his 2003 return without waiting for the written statement from Marilyn. On March 1, he receives the statement from Marilyn. He may not deduct the payments as alimony because he failed to get the required written statement before the return was filed.

Here's another example. Under the terms of their separation agreement, Robert must pay the mortgage, real estate taxes, and insurance premiums on a home owned solely by his ex-wife, Julia. Robert may deduct these payments as alimony. Julia must include the payments in her income, but she is entitled to claim deductions for the amount of the real estate taxes and mortgage interest if she itemizes her deductions.

- If the payor pays rent on the ex-spouse's apartment, the rent may be considered alimony. This must be stated in the divorce decree.
- If the payor pays the mortgage on the house owned by the ex-spouse, the payment might be considered to be alimony. This must be stated in the divorce decree.
- If the payor pays the mortgage on the house owned by the payor, the payment is not considered to be alimony.
- If the payee spouse owns the life insurance policy on the life of the payor, the payments made by the payor will qualify as alimony if so stated in the divorce decree.

The bottom line is: If the payor is making payments on something owned by the payor for the benefit of the ex-spouse, the payments do not qualify as alimony. If the payor makes payments on something owned by the ex-spouse, the payments do qualify as alimony if stated in the divorce decree.

   b. Payments made to maintain property owned by the payor-spouse might not qualify as alimony.

Assume the same facts from above, except that Robert and Julia own the residence as joint tenants. Since he has a 50% ownership interest in the home, Robert may deduct only one-half of the payments as alimony. However, he is entitled to claim deductions for interest with respect to his own half of the mortgage payments. Similarly,

Julia must report one-half of the payments as income and can only claim one-half of the deductible interest.

c. *Transfers of services do not qualify as alimony.*

Assume that Jake offered to mow his ex-wife's lawn all summer. He figured that would be worth $550 and it could be considered alimony. Sorry, Jake, it doesn't qualify.

2. There must be a written separation agreement or court order in order for the payments to qualify as alimony.

Craig and Sally are separated. Craig sends Sally a letter offering to pay her $400 a month alimony for three years. Sally feels this is a slap in the face since she raised his kids and kept his house clean for 18 years. She does not respond. Craig starts sending the $400 per month. Sally cashes the checks. Since there is no written agreement, he may not deduct the payments as alimony.

In another example, according to their divorce decree, Allen is to send Marian $750 per month in alimony for 10 years. Two years after their divorce, Marian loses her job and prevails on Allen's good nature to increase her alimony for six months until she can get started in a new job. He starts sending her an additional $200 per month. Keep in mind that since this was an oral agreement, not written, no post-decree modification was made and he may not deduct the additional $200.

Lesson learned? Get everything in writing!

3. The divorcing couple must not opt out of alimony treatment for federal income tax purposes.

Maintenance is taxable to the person who receives it and tax-deductible by the person who pays it (unless agreed upon otherwise. See taxable vs. non-taxable).

4. The divorcing couple may not be members of the same household at the time payment is made after the final decree.

Sometimes a couple gets divorced but neither can afford to move. They reach an agreement: She lives upstairs and he lives downstairs. He pays her maintenance but he cannot deduct it on his tax return. Since they live in the same house, it is not considered maintenance. However, for temporary alimony, the parties may be members of the same household.

5. The obligation to make payments must terminate upon the recipient's death.

The obligation ceases upon the death of the payor or the payee.

6. The ex-spouses may not file a joint tax return.

Many couples file for the year they got divorced. This is an error. The filing status is the status they have on December 31st of the year they are filing. If they are divorced during the year of 2003, on December 31, 2003 they are not married and may not file a joint return.

7. If any portion of the payment is considered to be child support, then that portion cannot be treated as alimony.

If alimony is reduced six months either side of the date upon which a child reaches the age of 18, 21, or the age of majority in their state, the amount of reduction is considered to be child support and not alimony.

TAXABLE VS. NON-TAXABLE

During the temporary separation period and until the divorce is final, the couple can decide whether the alimony payments should be considered taxable or non-taxable. Many times, any money that is paid to the spouse up to the time of permanent alimony is *not* considered maintenance. On the other hand, sometimes the temporary orders can consider it to be maintenance so it is taxable. Written agreements and good communication are essential here. Nothing should ever be assumed by either party!

FRONT-LOADING OF MAINTENANCE

The IRS has a rule that states that if the payor of alimony wants to deduct everything over $15,000 per year, payments must last for at least three years. The recapture rules were designed to prevent non-deductible property settlement payments from being deducted as alimony. The rules come into effect to the extent that alimony payments decrease annually in excess of $15,000 during the first three calendar years.

To the extent that the payor spouse has paid "excess alimony," the excess alimony is to be recaptured in the payor spouse's gross income beginning in the third year after divorce. The payee spouse is entitled to deduct the recaptured amount from gross income in the third year after divorce.

For example, Trish tells her husband Robert that after the divorce, she plans to go back to school for two years and finish her degree. Then she will be able to get a certain job that, after a year, will pay her $30,000 a year and she will no longer need alimony. She asks Robert if he will support her for those two years. He agrees. Her expenses for those two years, including school costs, are $60,000 the first year and $30,000 the second year.

A friend tells Robert about an IRS rule that says if he wants to deduct everything over $15,000, alimony must go for at least three years, but the rule doesn't stipulate as to the amount he must pay. Robert wants to deduct the whole amount so he offers to pay Trish $1,000 the 3rd year to satisfy the IRS ruling.

Here's what it looks like:

1st year	$60,000
2nd year	$30,000
3rd year	$ 1,000

However, the friend didn't tell Robert about the 2nd part of the IRS rule. *Some friend!* The IRS says that if the payments drop by more than $15,000 from one year to the next, there is tax recapture on the amount over $15,000. In Robert's case, the alimony dropped by $30,000 from year 1 to year 2, and by $29,000 from year 2 to year 3. Robert will have to pay tax recapture. **RESULT: Robert will add $50,500 to the gross income in the 3rd year and Trish will subtract $50,500 from the gross income.**

DECLINING MAINTENANCE

Keeping in mind the front-loading of maintenance rules, there are some advantages to structuring your alimony so that the payments decrease from year to year. For example, Lucy and Brian structured their divorce settlement so that Lucy would receive payments over a six year period. She would receive $2,000 per month for 2 years, while she was finishing her physical therapist degree. After completing her degree, she would get $1,500 per month for 2 years, while she was getting her business set up. During the final two years, she would get $1,000 per month. At the completion of six years, all payments would stop.

Lucy liked this arrangement because the gradual decline gave her a chance to get used to it and prepare to adjust her standard of living. In addition, she could tell how much she would need to work to replace the lost income.

Brian liked this arrangement because he could see and feel the decline of maintenance. And, he knew it wasn't going to go on forever. This is an important factor for the majority of individuals who are required to pay maintenance. There is a light at the end of the tunnel.

GUARANTEEING ALIMONY

Even though the divorce decree stipulates one spouse is to pay the other a certain amount of alimony for a certain period of time, it doesn't mean it will happen. There are several ways an ex-spouse can get out of making the payments. Fortunately, there are several ways to guard against this and guarantee the payments will be made. These include life insurance, disability insurance, and annuities, which will be discussed in more detail in Chapter 7.

Summary

- Get everything in writing! It is critical to the tax implications as well as to your income that you do not assume anything.
- If you are the lower-earning spouse or a stay-at-home custodial parent, you may be entitled to temporary support while your divorce proceedings are occurring. This is to be used to pay bills for everyday living expenses. It does not determine the amount you may receive after your case is final.
- Know and understand the difference between modifiable and non-modifiable alimony. In a modifiable outcome, it is common to see a final divorce order specify how much but not how long.

In this case, the door has been opened for future modifications to be made. If your alimony is non-modifiable, your divorce decree will state not only how much but also how long.

- Remember, alimony is taxable and tax-deductible. Some creativity can be used to offset both the higher and lower tax brackets of the recipients to end up with more dollars in the pockets of both spouses.

- In an effort to prevent couples from dividing their property by calling it alimony, the IRS has effected very specific tax rules. While the intricacies of this discussion are best left to your accountant, it is important to have a general understanding. The IRS will not classify alimony as alimony if it should drop from one year to the next by more than $15,000 within the first three years after divorce. If it does, the spouse taking the deduction will be forced to "re-capture" any tax deductions taken and pay them back to the IRS, appropriately called "Alimony Recapture."

chapter 6

CHILD SUPPORT

Jill and Jerry had two children, ages 5 and 7, when they divorced. No matter what Jill said, Jerry refused to include in their divorce agreement a clause which would increase child support each year by inflation. As the children grew up, they became more expensive and Jill was having trouble making ends meet. She contacted Jerry to tell him about her situation and how much the children's expenses had increased. Jerry said, "So sue me." So she did.

After being served with a court date, Jerry reluctantly agreed to increase child support to the amount according to the child support guidelines, using his current income and the children's current expenses, *not the income and expenses at the time of the divorce.*

Every parent knows first hand, the expense that goes into raising a child in this day and age. This becomes an even more daunting expense when two incomes suddenly become one. As we see in the above case, children often become pawns in the midst of divorce preceedings, whether intentional or not.

The United States Department of Agriculture Center for Nutrition Policy and Promotion released in their annual report, "Expenditures on Children by Families, 2003," estimates on the overall cost of raising a child across seven categories from birth to legal adult age:

Age of Child	Total	Housing	Food	Trans-portation	Clothing	Health care	Child care and education	Miscel-laneous†
Before-tax income: Less than $40,700 (Average = $25,400)								
0 - 2	$6,820	$2,620	$950	$800	$350	$500	$950	$650
3 - 5	6,970	2,580	1,050	770	340	480	1,080	670
6 - 8	7,040	2,500	1,360	900	380	550	640	710
9 - 11	6,990	2,250	1,620	970	420	600	390	740
12 - 14	7,840	2,510	1,710	1,100	710	610	270	930
15 - 17	7,770	2,030	1,850	1,480	630	650	450	680
Total	$130,290	$43,470	$25,620	$18,060	$8,490	$10,170	$11,340	$13,140
Before-tax income: $40,700 to $68,400 (Average = $54,100)								
0 - 2	$9,510	$3,540	$1,130	$1,190	$410	$660	$1,570	$1,010
3 - 5	9,780	3,510	1,310	1,160	400	630	1,740	1,030
6 - 8	9,730	3,420	1,670	1,290	450	720	1,110	1,070
9 - 11	9,600	3,180	1,960	1,360	490	780	730	1,100
12 - 14	10,350	3,440	1,980	1,490	830	790	530	1,290
15 - 17	10,560	2,950	2,200	1,880	740	830	920	1,040
Total	$178,590	$60,120	$30,750	$25,110	$9,960	$13,230	$19,800	$19,620
Before-tax income: More than $68,400 (Average = $102,400)								
0 - 2	$14,140	$5,620	$1,500	$1,660	$540	$760	$2,370	$1,690
3 - 5	14,470	5,590	1,700	1,630	530	730	2,580	1,710
6 - 8	14,240	5,500	2,050	1,760	580	830	1,770	1,750
9 - 11	14,040	5,260	2,380	1,840	630	900	1,240	1,790
12 - 14	14,850	5,520	2,500	1,960	1,050	900	950	1,970
15 - 17	15,350	5,040	2,630	2,380	950	950	1,670	1,730
Total	$261,270	$97,590	$38,280	$33,690	$12,840	$15,210	$31,740	$31,920

Table 6–1   ESTIMATED ANNUAL EXPENDITURES ON A CHILD BY HUSBAND-WIFE FAMILIES, OVERALL UNITED STATES, 2003.[1]

It is important to note that the above table illustrates the costs as applied to a husband–wife family. Let's take a look at those numbers when it becomes just one or the other:

Age of child	Single-parent households	Husband-wife households
0 - 2	$5,700	$6,820
3 - 5	6,440	6,970
6 - 8	7,230	7,040
9 - 11	6,710	6,990
12 - 14	7,210	7,840
15 - 17	7,960	7,770
Total	$123,750	$130,290

Table 6–2   COMPARISON OF ESTIMATED EXPENDI-TURES ON A CHILD BY SINGLE-PARENT AND HUS-BAND-WIFE FAMILIES, OVERALL UNITED STATES, 2003.[2]

It is worth noting that 83% of all single-parent families fall into the lower income group while only 33% of all husband–wife families do. The strenuous expense of raising a child on one income post-divorce is magnitude by the strain felt by two income, husband–wife families.

Parents are obligated to support their children, regardless of divorce. In a divorce situation, the non-custodial parent is usually ordered to pay some child support to the custodial parent from which the custodial parent pays the child's expenses. Most (90%) single-parent families in a survey conducted in 2003 were headed by a woman as such you'll notice that the case studies presented will refect that statistic.

In an effort to protect the child, the federal government has began to pass laws that would deprive states of certain Federal financial assistance unless those states implemented child support guidelines. All states now have child support guidelines that help the courts decide the amount of child support to be paid. Be sure to check in your own state for their particular guidelines. You most likely will be able to get software to automatically calculate the state guidelines for you.

However, the courts in each state still have the power to deviate from the child support guidelines (award a different amount). The state statutes tell what constitutes acceptable deviations. The parents can also agree to a different amount provided that the court approves the agreement.

Furthermore, some child support guideline formulas are based on the ratio of each parent's income and the percentage of time the child spends with each parent. Also consider the amount of alimony paid to the custodial parent. Let's take a look at an example of the application of an income ratio child support guidelines formula:

Paul's gross income is $4,300 a month and Becky's gross income is $900 a month; together they earn $5,200.

Paul	$4,300	83%
Becky	$ 900	17%
	$5,200	

Paul is earning 83 percent of the total and Becky is earning 17 percent. They have two children. The child support guidelines in their state for two children is $983. Using the guidelines, take 83 percent of the suggested monthly payment of $983 and you will determine that Paul owes Becky $813 in monthly child support *if he pays no alimony*.

But let's assume that he is going to pay her of $1,000 a month in alimony. At this point, you would then subtract the $1,000 from his income and add it to hers.

Paul	$4,300 − $1,000 = $3,300	63%
Becky	$ 900 + $1,000 = $1,900	37%
	$5,200 $5,200	

The totals stay the same but the percentages change. Now, his percentage is 63 percent. Using the same guidelines formula, multiply $983 by 63 percent. Paul will now be required to pay $624 per month instead of the $813.

> **The rule of thumb in this type of a formula is, as alimony *increases*, child support *decreases*.**

Unfortunately, the amount of child support paid is often less than the actual amount required to meet the needs of growing children. And secondly, many times the child support is not paid at all.

Many times, there is suspicion or anger from the husband. He thinks, "How can I be sure that my ex-wife will spend the money on the children. . . she probably will spend it on herself!" Child support is often based on income. So, obviously, it is based on some kind of lifestyle that was already established.

The husband thinks, "If I want my children to live in this kind of a house, I have to pay enough child support that will make that kind of house payment. That means my ex-wife is going to be there, too." So, many times, the husband will get angry because his ex-wife is getting alimony on top of child support. Or, if she is not getting alimony, he feels that she is living off the child support with none or very little of the money going to the children. However, there are many fathers who understand that for the children to live in the kind of house they're accustomed to, the wife has to be there with them.

Paul and Becky present a very simplistic example, illustrating that in real life, it's not always that cut and dry. In reality, there are several other factors that enter in, such as whether he is paying for childcare, health insurance, and/or education. These factors would make adjustments necessary to the child support amount. Also, if there are four children and three will live with the mother and one with the father, that would impact the financial picture. Another factor that affects the outcome is the percentage of time the children live with the father under the parenting schedule.

MODIFYING CHILD SUPPORT

What happens when circumstances change after the divorce is final? Say, the husband loses his job, the wife loses her job, one person becomes disabled, a settlement or judgment is awarded that was started when still married, or one of them wins the lottery.

> **Child support is always modifiable.**

The courts really try to protect the children. Therefore, even though couples with young children can agree on almost any settlement issue, unlike alimony payments, they cannot generally enter a binding agreement to waive the amount or duration of child support.

Child support can be modified unless there was an agreement to the contrary. They are usually modified for a substantial change of circumstances. How much of a change constitutes a "substantial" change in circumstance? If the income changes, in some states that might be enough to change the child support. According to the child support guidelines, if the amount changes by some minimum presumptive amount like 10–15%, then there are grounds for changing the child support payment.

There is an interesting issue. Assume there are two children and the child support level has been agreed upon. At some point, the older child decides to go live with Dad, for the summertime only. Since he's paying the full cost of supporting this child at his house (at least for several months), Dad says, "Now I only have to pay half the child support," and he sends a check for half the amount. Because it was not changed by a court order, in most states he still owes the whole amount and the ex-wife could force him to pay back that child support he did not pay.

Or suppose that both kids go to live with Dad during the summer. Dad says, "I do not have to pay any child support during the summer since both kids are living with me," but the court order says that he must pay so much every month. It does not say "nine months out of the year." Unless it is in the court order, he is liable for those payments, and his ex-wife could sue him for that money. It is important to have written agreements as circumstances change.

INCOME TAX CONSIDERATIONS

Child support payments differ more greatly than alimony payments when it comes to income tax considerations.

> **Child support payments <u>cannot</u> be deducted by the payor and can't be included in the income of the recipient.**

If the divorcing parents have only one child, that child can be counted as an exemption by only one parent in a given year. Unless otherwise specified, the exemption usually goes to the parent who has physical custody of the child for the greater portion of the calendar year, which means usually not the spouse making the child support payments.

The exemption can be traded back and forth year-to-year between the parents with a written waiver or IRS Form 8332 (be sure to ask your accountant for more details regarding this form). Once the custodial parent has executed the waiver, the noncustodial parent must attach the form to his or her income tax return. If the waiver is for more than one year, a copy of the form must be attached to the noncustodial parent's return for each year.

If the family has more than one child, the parents may divide up the exemptions. The children's Social Security numbers must be listed on each parent's tax return.

> **IMPORTANT:** If both parents claim the same child or children on their tax return, they are inviting an IRS audit.

For either parent to claim the exemption, the child must be in custody of at least one parent for more than one-half of the calendar year. If the child lives with a grandparent or someone other than a parent for more than one-half of the calendar year, neither parent may claim the exemption.

CHILD CONTINGENCY RULE

If any amount of alimony specified in the divorce agreement is reduced (a) upon the happening of any contingency related to the child or (b) at a time that can be clearly associated with a contingency related to the child, then the amount of the reduction will be treated as child support rather than alimony from the start.

In order to prevent re-characterization of the payments, it is necessary to avoid a reduction of alimony at a time associated with the occurrence of a child-related contingency. Sidestepping this trap is made easier by the fact that there are only two situations in which payments that would otherwise qualify as alimony will be presumed to be reduced at a time clearly associated with the occurrence of a contingency related to the child.

1. Six-Month Rule

The first situation occurs when the payments are to be reduced not more than six months before or after the date on which the child reaches age 18, 21 or the age of majority in their state.

Example: Michael is to pay Susan $2,000 per month in alimony. The amount of alimony is to be reduced to $1,000, beginning with the January 2002 payment. Their child, Todd, was born April 5, 1984 and will reach the age of majority (18) on April 5, 2002. The date six months before April 5, 2002 is October 5, 2001, and the date six months after is October 5, 2002. Thus, if there is any reduction in payments during the period from October 5, 2001 through October 5, 2002, it may be presumed that the amount of the reduction constitutes child support and not alimony.

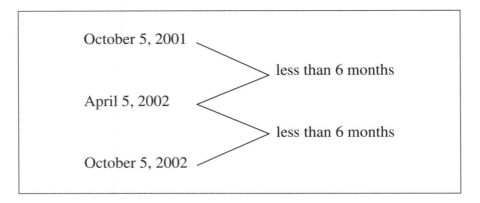

Thus, only $1,000 per month will qualify as alimony because the reduction in the payment falls within six months of a time associated with the occurrence of a child-related contingency.

2. Multiple Reduction Rule

The second situation is when there is more than one child. In this instance, if the payments are to be reduced on two or more occasions which occur not more than one year before or after each child reaches a certain age, then it is presumed that the amount of the reduction is child support. The age at which the reduction occurs must be between 18 and 24, inclusive, and must be the same for each of the children.

Example: Ralph is to pay Theresa $2,000 per month in alimony. Theresa has custody of their two children, Heidi and Thor. However, the payments are to be reduced to $1,500 per month on May 1, 2002 and to $1,000 per month on May 1, 2006. When the first reduction occurs, Heidi will be 20 years and 3 months old. On the date of the second reduction, Thor will be 21 years and 8 months old.

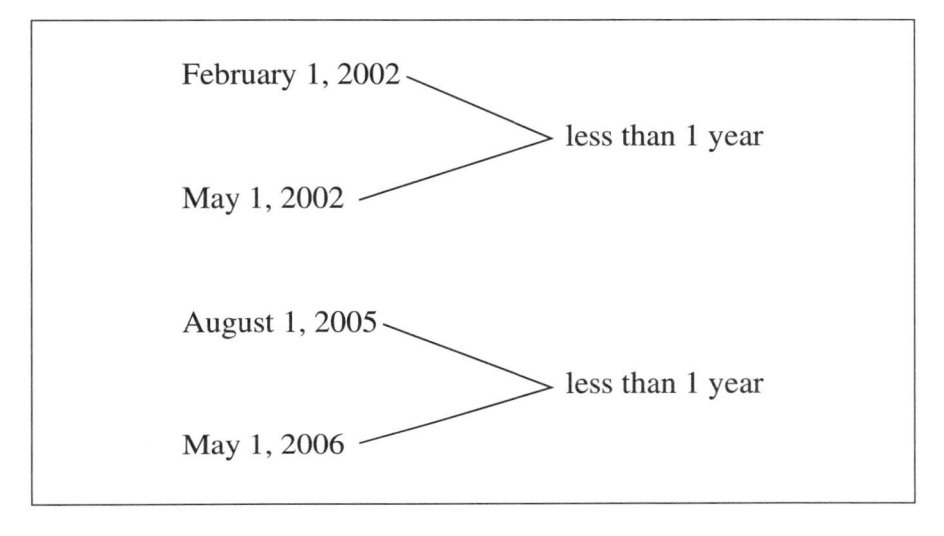

February 1, 2002

May 1, 2002

less than 1 year

August 1, 2005

May 1, 2006

less than 1 year

Under these facts, it is presumed that $1,000 of the payments constitutes child support, rather than alimony. Both reductions in payments occur not more than one year before or after each child reaches the age of 21 years.

Many attorneys will suggest that since "Joey is gradutating from high school in five years, let's give Mom alimony for five years." Or "Since Suzy is graduating in five years, let's give Mom alimony of $2,000 per month for those five years and then reduce it to $1,500 once Suzy has graduated." This is creating a serious tax problem for Dad. If the IRS considers the reduction of $500 a month to be child support, they will make it retroactive from the beginning (five years times $500). That would be $30,000 that Dad would have to pay tax recapture on!

CHILD CARE CREDIT

A custodial parent who pays child care expenses so that he or she can be gainfully employed may be eligible for a tax credit. To claim this credit, the parent must maintain a household that is the home of at least one child, and the day care expenses must be paid to someone who is not claimed as a dependent. Only the custodial parent is entitled to claim both the child and the dependent care credit. This is true even if the custodial parent does not claim the dependency exemption for the child.

Let's take a look at the following case: Carl's and Mandy's son Bret, age 4, lives with Mandy four days a week and with Carl three days a week. Both Carl and Mandy work outside the home and each pays one-half of the $5,000 per year that it costs to have Bret in daycare during the workweek. Mandy is entitled to claim a childcare credit for her share of the daycare expenses. Although Carl and Mandy each have custody of Bret for a significant portion of the week, Mandy is considered the custodial parent because Bret spends a greater percentage of time with her than he does with Carl.

HEAD OF HOUSEHOLD

A head-of-household filing status is available for those who are divorced (single), who provide more than one-half the cost of maintaining the household, and whose household is the principal home of at least one qualifying person for more than one-half of the year. A *qualifying person* is their child or any other person who qualifies as their dependent.

> NOTE: *In determining whether the home is the principal home of the child for more than one-half of the year, do not count absences for vacation, sickness, school, or military service as time spent away from home if it was reasonable to assume that the child would return to the home.*

Summary

- Child support is ALWAYS modifiable! Alimony as we saw in the last chapter may or may not be modifiable. In the interest of the child first and foremost, the courts will not allow us to take away the rights of the children. As such, child support is always modifiable.

- Know your child support guidelines. All states have child support guidelines. They are usually based on the incomes of both parents and the duration of time that the child (or children) spend with each.
- Be sure to consider the inclusion of a cost of living increase when finalizing your child support. We have shown in this chapter how expensive raising a child is — even more so as they get older! Make sure that you discuss including a cost of living increase each year for child support in your settlement.

Notes

1. "Expenditures on Children by Families, 2003," United States Department of Agriculture Center for Nutrition Policy and Promotion, Miscellaneous Publication Number 1528-2003.
2. "Expenditures on Children by Families, 2003," United States Department of Agriculture Center for Nutrition Policy and Promotion, Miscellaneous Publication Number 1528-2003.

PART 4

ADDITIONAL THINGS TO CONSIDER

chapter 7

INSURANCE

Joan was receiving $400 per month in alimony from her ex–husband Jerry. The court had ordered Jerry to carry life insurance on his life, payable to Joan as long as alimony was being paid. After three years, Jerry was tired of making the insurance payments so he stopped and the insurance was canceled. Nobody knew about it until one year later. Jerry was in a tragic car accident and died two weeks later of complications from his injuries. Alimony came to an abrupt halt and there was no life insurance! Yes, Jerry was in contempt of court but it didn't make any difference now, because his estate was insufficient to pay the claim of the wife.

Throughout section 2, you read about career assets that need to be considered as dividable property. In this chapter, we will cover two additional career assets: health insurance and life insurance.

HEALTH INSURANCE AND COBRA

In the traditional marriage where the husband is the main wage earner, one concern is maintaining health insurance for the ex-wife after divorce.

It is not uncommon for women over 40 years of age to develop severe health problems. Some become almost uninsurable, at least at a reasonable cost. This is a real concern where, all of a sudden, they are on their own and responsible for acquiring health insurance often without the means to pay for it.

The Older Women's League (OWL) worked hard to get the Consolidated Omnibus Budget Reconciliation Act (COBRA) law passed in 1986. It allows women to continue to get health insurance from their ex-husband's company (if it has at least 20 employees) for three years after the divorce. The normal COBRA provision states that, if an employee is fired or leaves a job, he or she can get health insurance from that company for 18 months. However, in a divorce, it is extended to three years or 36 months.

Assume that Sara and Bob have been married for 12 years before their divorce. Sara decides to continue health insurance under COBRA. She *must* pay the premium as agreed for if she misses a premium payment, the health insurance company can drop her and they do not need to reinstate her. So, she must pay that premium on time. Typically, Sara will not get the discounted group rate but will be charged the full rate. It is important to shop for health insurance, even though the COBRA provision may supply a quick solution to health care coverage, it may not be the best. It may be purchased at a lesser cost somewhere else.

In fact, one Financial Divorce Specialist that I know makes it a priority to talk to all of her female clients about health insurance. All of her clients over the age of 40 are encouraged to explore other options. They are told, "I would advise that you shop for health insurance because if you can match the rate from your husband's company or get a lower premium with another company, you should buy your own. Then if something happens, as long as you pay your premiums, you are covered. Otherwise, at the end of three years, COBRA drops you, and then you have to start shopping for your own insurance. By that time, you might be uninsurable and not able to find insurance."

Most states have insurance for those who are uninsurable and cannot get health insurance any other way. As may be expected, this insurance is very costly. It is better to look ahead and get individual health insurance for a lower premium while you are still healthy than to gamble that you will still be healthy three years later.

Is health insurance a marital asset? In recent years, some divorce lawyers have started to consider this an asset ever since the Financial Accounting Standards Board in 1993 began requiring employers to calculate the present value of the future benefits and show a liability for that value in their financial reports. If the benefits are a liability to the employer, there's a good argument they *should* also be an asset to the employee.

LIFE INSURANCE

Since maintenance usually stops upon the death of the payor, the stream of payments can be covered by life insurance on the life of the payor if there is no other adequate source of security to fund the future stream of income. This should be part of the final divorce settlement.

I recommend that the wife own the life insurance policy and make the premium payments. This prevents any changes in the policy without her knowledge. I also strongly advise the wife, if she can afford it, to have the life insurance build cash value. Then, the cash account within the policy is hers to do with whatever she wishes. She may even use it for retirement. She can borrow from it at any time or cancel the policy and use the cash.

Another recommendation is to make sure that, if new insurance is needed, it be applied for before the divorce is final. Then, if he cannot pass the physical and cannot get new insurance, there is still time to modify the final settlement to make up for this possibility.

For example, Alex agreed to buy a life insurance policy to insure his alimony payments to Sarah. After the divorce was final, he applied for the insurance and took his health exam. He was found to be uninsurable. If Sarah had known this before the divorce, she could have had her attorney ask for a different settlement. Now, it's too late.

If the court orders the husband to purchase insurance to cover alimony and/or child support, those premium payments are treated like alimony for tax purposes and he can deduct them from his taxable income. Likewise, the wife will need to declare them as taxable income, unless the parties agree in their separation agreement to exempt the payment from the alimony tax treatment.

DISABILITY INSURANCE

A second way to guarantee the stream of maintenance income is to have disability insurance on the payor's ability to earn income. Assume, for example, that a husband is to pay his ex-wife $1,200 per month based on his salary of $6,000 per month. Then he becomes disabled. If he had disability insurance, he might then receive $4,000 per month tax-free and could continue making alimony payments. If he had no insurance and no income, he would probably go back to court and ask to have the payments modified.

The ex-wife cannot own the disability policy but she may make the payments on it so that she knows it stays in force. She will also, in that case, be notified of any changes made in the policy.

ANNUITY

A third way to guarantee that you receive alimony is to have the payor buy an annuity that pays an amount per month that equals the maintenance payment.

Assume that Ted buys a $200,000 annuity that will pay out $850 per month (the agreed-upon alimony payment) in interest only. If the payment represents interest-only payments, they are taxable to him as income, but deductible by him as alimony. His wife Judy will pay taxes on the payments. This way, the payment is always made on time, the payor does not need to worry about it, the recipient does not have to worry about it, and the principal can still belong to the payor.

If the agreed-upon alimony payment is $1,000 per month and Ted chooses to annuitize the annuity and receive $1,000 per month, part of the payment will be taxable to him, say $850, but he will be able to deduct the whole $1,000 as alimony payments. At the end of the term of alimony, he will continue to receive the $1,000 per month.

Summary

- Don't jump the gun on canceling your insurance too soon. Suppose you are the beneficiary of your spouse's insurance and it is cancelled? Two results may occur: (1) Your spouse may die before the divorce is final and there are no proceeds or (2) the court orders your spouse to carry insurance to cover alimony — now that your spouse is older, it may be too costly to get the required insurance.
- It is extremely important to protect the stream of income you'll need to survive as you make this transition in your life. Alimony stops upon the death of the payor. Therefore, it is important to

ensure that you protect that income stream with life insurance on the payor's life.

- If you can afford it, consider self-insuring. While in divorce, COBRA allows for up to 36 (or 3 years) of continued health insurance. It is important to consider getting your own. After the 36-month period, you run the risk of having become uninsurable and, therefore, they do not have to continue insuring you. If you had bought your own, as long as you pay your premiums, you are covered.

chapter 8

SOCIAL SECURITY: HERS, HIS OR HIS? HIS, HERS OR HERS?

Maude's first husband Joe died. At age 58, she meets a wonderful widower and talk of marriage soon follows. They want to get remarried but Maude soon realized that she would loose her entitlement to all of Joe's (deceased spouse) Social Security benefits when she turned age 60.

This may explain why so many senior citizens are choosing to live together, unmarried...

NOTE: *For all the examples in this chapter, we will assume that the wife was the lower-earning spouse. In real life, the husband could be the lower-earning spouse, in which case all rules would apply to him.*

You may or may not know that if a couple has been married for 10 years or longer and they get divorced, the wife is entitled to half the husband's Social Security, provided certain provisions are met:

1. The husband is entitled to receive Social Security benefits.
2. They had been married for 10 years before the divorce became final.
3. The wife is not married.
4. The wife is age 62 or over.
5. The wife is not entitled to a retirement benefit, which equals or exceeds one-half the husband's benefit.

Since this rule does not diminish the amount the husband receives at retirement, he usually doesn't worry about this.

A wife who is age 62 or over and who has been divorced for at least two years, will be able to receive benefits based on the earnings of a former husband, regardless of whether the former husband has retired or applied for benefits.

If the wife chooses to start receiving benefits at age 62, the benefit that she would receive at age 65 is reduced by 20%. If the wife chooses to receive the reduced benefit at age 62, she is not entitled to the full benefit upon reaching age 65.

Assume the husband will get $750 a month when he retires. If they have been married for 10 years or longer, she would be able to get $375 (half of the husband's benefit) at age 65.

Husband	$750
Wife	$375

What if he gets remarried? If he is married to his second wife for 10 years and they get divorced, wife 2 gets $375, wife 1 gets $375, and he still gets $750. The limit is four marriages! As long as he is married to each one for a period of 10 years or longer, they each get half of his Social Security benefit.

Husband	$750
Wife 1	$375
Wife 2	$375

One of the reasons why Social Security is in so much financial trouble is that the fund is covering and paying for items that it was not originally designed to do.

What if the wife gets remarried? If she is married at retirement time, she looks to her current husband for her benefit. But if she has been married to husband # 2 for 10 years and they get divorced, she is entitled to half of husband # 1's benefits or half of husband # 2's benefits. She has a choice.

Husband # 1	$750	Husband # 2	$600
Wife	$375	Wife	$300

If husband # 2 is entitled to $600 at retirement, she obviously will choose the benefits from husband # 1. They are more.

Assume she begins working after the kids are raised and that by the time she retires, she is going to be able to earn $450 from her own Social Security account. Now, she has the choice at retirement time of taking $450 from her own account, $300 from husband # 2's account, or $375 from husband # 1's account. She can only have one — hers, his or his. Obviously, she would take her own account, which would pay her $450 per month.

What if they get divorced and he dies? The wife is entitled to full widow's benefits (100 percent of the deceased husband's benefits) if:

1. The deceased husband was entitled to Social Security benefits.
2. They had been married for 10 years before the divorce became final.
3. The widow is age 60 or over or is between ages 50 and 60 and disabled.
4. The widow is not married.
5. The widow is not entitled to a retirement benefit that is equal to or greater than the deceased husband's benefit.

Wife # 2 also gets full widow's benefits if she meets the above five requirements.

A widow's remarriage **after** age 60 *will not prevent* her from being entitled to widow's benefits on her prior deceased husband's earnings.

A widow's remarriage **before** age 60 *will prevent* entitlement to widow's benefits unless the subsequent marriage ends, whether by death, divorce, or annulment. If the subsequent marriage ends, the widow may become entitled or reentitled to benefits on the prior deceased spouse's earnings, beginning with the month the subsequent marriage ends.

Social Security benefits payable to the ex-wife are reduced by governmental retirement payments to the husband. These payments are based on his own earnings in employment, not covered by Social Security on the last day of such employment. The reduction is two-thirds of the pension. Thus, the wife's benefit is reduced $2 for every $3 of the government pension.

Summary

- The magic number is 10! If you have been married for ten years or longer when you get divorced, the lower earning spouse can get half the higher earning spouse's Social Security benefit.
- Hers, his or his? His, hers or hers? You can get your own benefit or half of your spouse's benefit — whichever is higher. This holds true even if you have been married twice. You have a choice — buy you can only get one benefit.

chapter 9

CREDIT, DEBT AND BANKRUPTCY: THE GOOD, THE BAD AND THE UGLY

Tracy and Paul were married for 8 years, during which time Tracy ran her credit cards to the limit with her compulsive spending. The court held Tracy solely responsible for paying the $12,000 in credit card debt. After the divorce, however, Tracy didn't change her ways and was unable to pay off her debt. The credit card companies came after Paul, who ended up paying them off.

Note: One solution would have been to pay off the credit cards with assets at the time of divorce or for Paul to have received more property to offset this possibility.

DEBT

As you read earlier, property is classified as marital and separate. The same classifications apply to debt. In general, in many states both parties are responsible for any debts incurred during the marriage — it does not matter who really spent the money. When the property is divided up during the divorce, the person who gets the asset usually also gets the responsibility for any loans against that asset.

It's in your best interests to pay off as many debts as possible before or at the time of the final agreement. To do so, you could use liquid assets such as bank accounts, stocks, or bonds. It may make sense to sell assets to accumulate some extra cash. The best assets to sell include extra cars, vacation homes, and excess furniture.

If you can't pay off the debts, then the agreement must state who will pay which debt and within what period of time. However, the parties are still personally liable to the third party creditor regardless of what the court order says.

There are generally four types of debt to consider:

- Secured debt
- Unsecured debt
- Tax debt
- Divorce expense debt

SECURED DEBT

Secured debt includes the mortgage on the home or other real estate, loans on cars, trucks, and other vehicles. It should be made very clear in the separation agreement who will pay which debt. If one spouse fails to make a payment on a debt that is secured by an asset, the creditor can pursue the other spouse.

UNSECURED DEBT

Unsecured debt includes credit cards, personal bank loans, lines of credit, and loans from parents and friends. These debts may be divided equitably. The court also considers who is better able to pay the debt in the context of the full financial settlement.

Financial advisors, lawyers and clients all need to be aware that even though something is agreed to and included in the divorce decree, it doesn't mean that it will happen as planned. Often, the legal decision and the financial outcome are two very different things.

TAX DEBT

Just because the divorce settlement is final doesn't mean you are exempt from possible future tax debt. For three years after the divorce, the IRS can perform a random audit of your joint tax return. In addition, the IRS can question a joint return — if it has good cause to do so — for *seven years*. It can also audit a return whenever it feels fraud is involved. To avoid potential tax costs, the divorce agreement should have provisions that spell out what happens if any additional interest, penalties, or taxes are found, as well as where the money comes from to pay for an audit. However, if a joint tax return was filed, each of you is individually responsible to the IRS.

DIVORCE EXPENSE DEBT

At times, either you or your spouse may have paid some divorce expenses before the divorce process was officially started.

You will accrue costs during the divorce process, including court filing fees, appraisals, mediation, and attorneys. Other less obvious expenses are accounting, financial planning, and counseling. The separation agreement needs language that states who is responsible for these expenses.

CREDIT

A creditor cannot close an account just because the account holder's marital status has changed. An exception would be if there were a proven inability or unwillingness to pay. However, the creditor can require a new application if the original application was based on only the other spouse's financial statement. The creditor must allow use of the account while the new application is being reviewed.

If you have a good credit history and the necessary income, you should have little or no problem opening new accounts in your name only. If, however, you were unemployed during the marriage and never had a credit card in your name, you may need a cosigner.

You may still be responsible for joint accounts even after the divorce is final. You should see to it that prior to the final agreement, all joint accounts are paid off and closed, and that new accounts are started in your name.

Also be warned about running up charge account bills as part of divorce planning or retaliation. If it can later be proven that these expenditures were not agreed upon jointly (or they were not for necessities such as food, housing, clothing, or health care) they may not be considered joint debt, depending on the state law and the case.

> **Creditors don't care how the separation agreement divides responsibility for debt. Each person is liable for the full amount of debt on joint cards until the bill is paid.**

BANKRUPTCY

The word *bankruptcy* strikes fear in the hearts of many people — especially those going through divorce. Many wives who are trying to decide whether it is better to ask for alimony or a property settlement note are caught in indecision. Perhaps the husband has threatened to either leave the country if he has to pay alimony or to file bankruptcy if he has to pay a property settlement note. Let's look at some of the rules of bankruptcy as they apply in divorce situations.

There are two types of bankruptcy available: Chapter 13 (which allows you to develop a pay-off plan over a three-year period) or Chapter 7 (which allows you to liquidate all of your assets and use the proceeds to pay off debts, erasing the debts which cannot be paid in full).

Chapter 7 bankruptcy forgives all unsecured debts and requires the forfeiture of all assets over certain minimum protected amounts. Creditors have the right to repossess their fair share of the assets. The net proceeds from the sale of assets are divided pro rata among the creditors.

Chapter 13 bankruptcy may preserve the assets and allow the debtor to pay off all the secured debt, as well as a portion of the unsecured debt, and discharge the rest of the unsecured debt. The debtor needs to make payments under a plan.

Here are some things to remember:

- If a spouse files bankruptcy before, during, or after divorce, the creditors will seek out the other spouse for payment — no matter what was agreed to in the separation agreement.
- While the couple is still married, they can file for bankruptcy jointly. This will eliminate all separate debts of the husband, separate debts of the wife, and all jointly incurred marital debts.

Certain debts cannot be discharged in bankruptcy. These include child support, maintenance, some student loans, and recent taxes.

Promissory notes or property settlement notes, especially unsecured notes, are almost always wiped out in bankruptcy. Some secured notes, depending on the property that secures them, can also be discharged.

As an example, say Sam and Trudy divided all their assets. However, to achieve a 50/50 division, Sam still owed Trudy $82,000. Sam signed a property settlement note to pay Trudy the $82,000 over a 10-year period at 7 percent interest. After the divorce, Sam filed for bankruptcy and listed the property settlement note as one of his debts. Trudy never received a penny of the money that was due her.

Summary

- It does not matter who spent the money. In many states, both parties are responsible for any debts incurred during the marriage.
- Just because the divorce settlement is final doesn't mean the parties are exempt from possible future tax debt. For three years after the divorce, the IRS can perform a random audit of the divorced parties' joint tax return.
- If the spouses hold charge accounts jointly, they will both have the same credit history.
- While the word *bankruptcy* strikes fear in the hearts of many people — especially those going through divorce — certain debts cannot be discharged in bankruptcy. These include child support, maintenance, some student loans, and recent taxes.

PART 5

THE PROCESS

ALTERNATIVES TO TRIAL: EXPLORING YOUR DIVORCE OPTIONS USING A SETTLEMENT AGREEMENT

Ed and Sue had divided all their assets but one. Ed didn't want Sue to have any part of his "poker savings account," a $19,000 savings account representing his winnings from poker over a 12-year period. Sue insisted that half of it was hers, so Ed hired an expensive attorney and went to court rather than give in. He ended up spending $22,000 in fees — but he kept Sue from getting his savings account!

Care needs to be taken that couples who want to work out a settlement with a minimum of stress don't get caught up in their own knock-off of *The War of the Roses* starring Michael Douglas, Kathleen Turner and Danny DeVito. Unfortunately, once the flames have been ignited, the only person who will ever win is the attorney. Contrary to popular misconception, most couples don't want to use their financial resources for a court battle. Divorce is a highly volatile and emotional environment that as we saw in the case of Ed and Sue can easily spin out of control. It is important that you and your spouse consider utilizing a neutral third party, whose only gain is in helping you to navigate this highly stressful time in your life with as much ease as possible.

WHAT IS MEDIATION?

Simply put, mediation is where you and your spouse meet with a neutral third party to try and reach an amicable settlement. Mediation is a relatively new process that is quickly gaining recognition world wide for its ability to generate successful accomplishments.

> **This chapter would not be complete without mentioning the pioneer and forefather of divorce mediation, Gary J. Friedman, J.D. He realized in 1976 that there was a better way to resolve the issues surrounding divorce. Friedman shifted his focus "from doing battle to helping people work together to make decisions regarding their lives rather than making one party a winner and the other a loser."**

Let's get an expert's opinion on how the process works, the types and styles of negotiation that takes place and the importance of effective listening. Christine Coates, J.D. is no stranger to the mediation process. As a nationally known trainer and speaker on mediation, she has been mediating divorce cases in Colorado since 1984. In addition, we'll hear from Michael Caplan, J.D. Michael has been training mediators since 1988 and is a mediator himself. Knowing what to expect in the process can ease much of the anxiety that couples face when choosing mediation as their path to negotiating an agreement.

> *Christine:*
>
> "What is mediation? Mediation is a process where a neutral person works with the divorcing parties to devise solutions that work for both of them. The mediator is a neutral, impartial person who doesn't take sides, has no interest in the outcome of the mediation, does not give or make decisions for the parties, and does not give legal advice. This is an important point. Even if an attorney is working as a mediator, it would be unethical for him or her — as the mediator — to give legal advice. However, the mediator can give legal *information*.
>
> **"In the mediation process, the goal is to work with the parties and help them identify the**

issues. Together, they uncover what each party really needs in order to have a fair settlement. To do that, all the facts are presented that are necessary to making an informed decision, and the mediator helps both parties resolve the issues to their satisfaction in a way that's fair to them.

"Mediation is generally a voluntary process. The courts may order people to enter mediation, but the courts cannot order people to settle. Across the country, the courts are favoring mediation and ordering people to participate to make sure that they've had a chance to talk together before they end up in court.

"The mediator's job is to be a facilitator and to help the couple work together. The mediator has no authority to force a decision upon them. Mediation is not therapy, even though some divorce mediators are therapists. It is not meant to work out what went wrong in their marriage, nor is it arbitration (where one person makes a decision for the couple). It is a very different method of resolving disputes.

"Mediation is generally confidential depending on the state law. If confidential, the mediator cannot be called into court to testify against either of the parties or to tell the court or the judge what has occurred in the mediation session. However, each state has its own rules on this issue. Mediation should be a safe forum where the couple can talk about proposed solutions with each other, resolve their disputes, and perhaps come up with a settlement.

"The goal of mediation is to get past the positions that people come in with and work toward, what they really need in order to be satisfied with an agreement and to walk out with a fair and satisfying agreement.

"How does mediation work? There is a fairly predictable process although mediators have different styles and approaches. First of all, when two people visit the mediator, he or she gets to know them and spends some time telling them about mediation and how it works.

The mediator asks them to sign a contract telling them what is expected from them and what they can expect from the mediator, and how the fees are charged.

"Before beginning the mediation session in earnest, it is good to set ground rules. Two basic rules are:

1. Each person has the right to speak without being interrupted by the other.
2. Neither spouse should put down the other or resort to name-calling.

"The parties are told that the goal of mediation is to resolve their disputes, but the mediator is not going to do that for them. It is going to be their job and they are going to have to make their own decisions. The mediator will help them with what they need to know, what data they need to gather, and what information they need to bring to the table. He or she will help them figure out what to do and what agreements they need to reach. But the mediator is not going to reach decisions for them.

"After meeting with them initially, some mediators meet with each person separately to get a sense of what each of them is feeling, what their fears are, and what's been going on with them that they may not feel comfortable talking about in front of the other. The mediator finds out what it is that they really need to have happen to feel that they have had a fair agreement. (However, some mediators never meet with the parties alone. This depends on the style of the mediator.)

"After meeting with each alone, the three get back together to set the agenda. The mediator will have helped each of them to sort out the issues so they can decide which topics to talk about, such as property division, child support, maintenance, and so on. Then they select an issue on which to begin working.

"Sometimes, the mediator may decide which issue to start with. He or she may choose the issue that seems the easiest especially if there is an issue on which they agree even though they may not have told each other. Choosing that issue will help them get a quick agreement right off the bat so they can reinforce their ability to continue to work together to make future agreements. However, sometimes they come in with issues that demand immediate attention. If they don't deal with them that first day, mediation may go nowhere. In those cases, the process may start with a tough issue.

"After agreeing to the ground rules, they start the negotiating process. However, the couple often can't simply jump in and resolve issues. Many times, they first need to gather the information that is needed to make a decision. They need to know what their financial situation is, how much they spend, what the IRAs are worth, and so on. They will begin by filling out the standard financial affidavit form that is used in their state in compiling such information. Next, they will list all the property. A Financial Divorce Specialist can help them gather all this information.

"Once all the information is on the table, the mediator can start generating options for settlement."

THE NEGOTIATING PROCESS

After the ground rules are set and the couple has all their financial data in order, it is time to start the negotiating process. Let's hear from Michael as he explains how a mediator typically approaches it.

Michael:

"There are basically two ways of negotiating or bargaining. The first method is *positional bargaining*. Positional bargaining starts with the solution. One party proposes a solution and the other makes an offer. There are counteroffers until, somewhere along the line, they hit on something that is successful and that works for both of them.

"While this process sounds very calm and fair, there often is an undercurrent of selfishness. One spouse goes in with a low-ball offer and the other comes in with their high-ball offer. Somewhere in the middle, hopefully they will find a place where they are going to meet and where they think they are okay. Both people are also working from the notion that the "pie" is limited. They think, 'There is only so much here and I have to get as much as I can. I am looking to win and for me to win, you have to lose. That is my goal. I want to win as much as possible. For me to do that, you have to lose as much as possible.'

"Secondly, there is *interest-based bargaining*. It starts with parties educating each other about their interests. So instead of saying, 'I must have this,' they say, 'I need this because this is what it will do for me.'

"It is based instead on 'the pie is not limited, there is enough there for what we both want and need.' Now, that may not always be true but that is the assumption that they start with. It is based on the premise that all our needs may not be met 100% in the way we mainly would like them to be, but they will be met in a way we can live with.

"For example, when the wife says, 'I need to have the house,' the mediator shouldn't say, 'You can't have the house if you can't afford it.' What the mediator could say is, 'Tell me more about why that is important to you.' Then she might tell you that, 'Well, the house is the only asset in which I have any money and it's the only asset I can get some money out of.' This response gives valuable information.

"When the parties come in with their information, we often start getting information disagreements. I might say, 'It looks like we need to determine the value of the house. What process do you want to use to determine what the value of that real estate is?' If they don't have a clear idea of what this means, I will suggest they get some help, such as from their own financial planner or other expert."

Christine agrees with the importance of interest-based bargaining.

Christine:

"How do people negotiate? It means they turn from a position-based style to an interest-based style. A position is the specific proposal or solution that a party adopts to meet his or her interests or needs. It is the party's solution to what they would really like to see happen. They want the other party to say yes or no.

"This differs from the interest-based style, which is the concern or what the party wants to accomplish through his or her position. **In almost every mediation, people come in with a position — they are very strong in what they want. But when the mediator starts probing, he or she finds that there is more than just that position. There is a need underneath it.** When anyone is stuck in a position, there is not a lot of room to negotiate.

"If a the wife says, 'I must have $2,000 per month maintenance and that's final.' Or the husband says, 'I'll pay $2,000 per month for five years. That's it. No more.' Neither party can go very far with that. But when they start talking about what is underneath all that — is it for school, is it to meet reasonable needs, is it to support the household until the children are out of school — there emerges room to negotiate."

THE ROLE OF LISTENING IN MEDIATION

True, active listening is a big part of the mediator's job. However, it's not just the mediator that can benefit from active listening.

According to Michael, "Effective listening is the other part of what we are doing. How many times do we think we already know what the other person is trying to say? It takes energy to listen and you need to focus on the speaker. If I have my own talk going on in my head, I am going to have a hard time being able to hear. We need to check out what we think we heard to find out if we have it right and then we need to let the other party know that we really heard them.

Michael:

"So many times, women in the more traditional marriages have not really been heard. Their mate really has not listened them to. The anger and resentment are there and sometimes it gets suppressed, so when it does come out it spills out more like a volcano and involves issues that really may not be important.

"Listening is different from problem-solving or giving advice. How many times have you gone to a friend and started talking to them and they said, 'Yeah, I had that problem once and this is what I did' or 'You know, if you would only do this that would do it.'

"What I want to do when I am active listening is to feedback the feeling and content. 'So you are really upset and a bit anxious about the fact that I came in late and you were worried about whether I was going to show up.' Look for what the feeling is and give back the feeling first and try to match intensity."

Christine agrees.

Christine:

"The mediator (nor the couple involved) can never assume that he or she heard what the couple means. For example, when women listen, many nod their head and say 'Uh-huh, uh-huh.' Men just sit and listen, rarely showing any facial expression, much less head movement. When men hear women saying, 'Uh-huh, uh-huh,' they think the woman is agreeing with them when the woman is actually only indicating that she is listening. When men sit and listen but don't say anything, women think the man is not listening. This gender difference in listening styles leads to miscommunication.

"**Listening involves asking questions to make things more clear, but it is not interviewing. People want to know that they are being heard and then will get the facts afterwards.** *Listening is not problem-solving.* It is not hearing what someone has to say and then jumping in with, 'Here's what you need to do. I know exactly how you can fix this problem.'"

COMMON MISTAKES IN ACTIVE LISTENING

Too many times we try to solve someone's problem without actually having heard his or her need. So what can we do to improve our listening skills? We've put together a list of common mistakes that people tend to make in active listening:

- Trying to solve the problem instead of focusing on what the other person is trying to say. Each person has the inherent ability to solve his or her own problems.
- Telling the other person that we understand.
- Continuing to ask closed-end questions instead of open-ended questions.

WHERE TO FIND A MEDIATOR

When you need a mediator, how do you find one? Being an attorney or therapist does not necessarily mean they would make a good mediator. Unfortunately, few states have certification requirements or a minimum amount of training necessary to become a mediator.

Mediators need different sets of skills, especially in handling conflict. Before hiring a mediator, check out his or her qualifications. It's important to know who has had training and experience. Ask. The minimum amount of training acceptable is 40 hours. There are mediation organizations in each state. Check your telephone book.

WHEN MEDIATION MAY NOT WORK

Some people feel that they are not ideal candidates for mediation because they can't talk to each other, they can't communicate, or they're in high conflict. Well, almost everyone going through divorce is in that situation. People in divorce are often confused. They know how to push each other's buttons. It is the rare couple that can really communicate even when they're going through a divorce.

Even so, there are some couples who should not mediate. For example, people going through a divorce where there has been domestic violence should not be in mediation because there has been power imbalance in that relationship. Or in situations where there is mental illness or substance abuse, mediation will probably not work. If there is even some type of substance abuse going on, the person should not be in mediation. The substance abuse is an indication that one of the parties does not have the power to do what they need to do. If they are addicted to a substance, the likelihood is that they also are unable to follow through on agreed-upon solutions.

Another area in which mediation should not be used is when one or both of the parties are ignoring the children's best interests.

In addition, if the clients want the mediator to make the decisions or if one party seems to be giving in on all matters and you sense this was the norm in their relationship, these may not be good parties for mediation. Here's an example: Norm and Donna came in to see the mediator. The one item that raised a red flag was the fact that Norm had done a lot of work in forming a software company. Because of his work and some contracts that he had put together, he had signed agreements that promised him bonuses for the next five years. Depending on profits, these agreements could give him up to $1 million per year for five years. Donna said that she had no right to those because they would come in after the divorce. She constantly looked at him for approval of what she was saying. The mediator asked Norm if he felt those were marital property and he guessed they were. The mediator then asked Donna again if she agreed that they were marital property. She looked timid and repeated that she wouldn't want to take those away from Norm. Finally, the mediator had to advise Donna to see an attorney before they could proceed further. She needed to know her legal rights.

ARBITRATION

A second option for couples not wishing to go to court is arbitration. Often times, there is confusion between mediation and arbitration.

What is the difference between mediation and arbitration? In mediation, two parties share the decision. In arbitration, the power to decide is solely with the arbitrator. The two parties meet with the arbitrator, present each of their positions (much like mediation), and then the arbitrator makes the decision for them, which is binding (in most states).

Some couples want to arbitrate because they disagree and can't seem to move past their deadlock. They feel that the only possible solution is to hand over the power of deciding to a third party. If the parties agree ahead of time that the arbitration will be binding, they are guaranteed a resolution of their dispute. It can be both efficient and informal, and thus a good alternative to going to court. Its effectiveness depends on the arbitrator's ability to gain a clear enough understanding of the issues to make a wise decision.

Arbitration is especially tempting for people who think they are right, because they are sure that their position will be vindicated by the arbitrator. And because people who feel they are right often see the other person as wrong, it is easy for them to see the process as one that will end in victory for themselves and defeat of the other. The fact that they agree to turn over their decision-making power tends to encourage the parties to skew the information they present to the arbitrator, painting their own views with righteousness and trying to invalidate the other's position. Defending one's position is a natural human tendency that is enhanced when one does not have the power to decide.

COLLABORATIVE DIVORCE

A third alternative that has gained recent popularity is Collaborative Divorce; a new and highly effective divorce method that utilizes Collaborative Law. Teams of professionals trained in the Collaborative Divorce interdisciplinary method are springing up all over the United States. Let's take a look at some of the most common questions asked in regards to Collaborative Divorce:

1. What is Collaborative Divorce?
Collaborative Divorce is a team approach to divorce that includes gender-balanced divorce coaches, neutral financial specialists, Collaborative Law attorneys and, when needed, child specialists. Divorcing families obtain professional help from specialists in the psychotherapy, financial,

and legal fields to help them settle their case. Each team member assists the family in his/her area of expertise, and then works integratively with other team members and with the collaborative law attorneys who help families reach viable divorce settlements. The team teaches communication skills so that parents can communicate better with each other and in the future around their children's needs. Finances are addressed, budgets are created, and financial skills taught where needed. Although more professionals are involved in collaborative divorce cases, the cost is lower for the family overall because the family receives specific and focused divorce assistance which allows for more productive work when meeting with their attorneys to reach settlement. Collaborative Law attorneys are the legal professionals on a Collaborative Divorce team.

2. What is Collaborative Law?
Collaborative Law is a new dispute resolution model in which both parties to the dispute retain separate, specially trained lawyers whose only job is to help them settle the dispute. All participants agree to work together respectfully, honestly, and in good faith to try to find "win-win" solutions to the legitimate needs of both parties. No one may go to court or even threaten to do so, and if that should occur, the Collaborative Law process terminates and both lawyers are disqualified from any further involvement in the case.

3. What is the Difference between Collaborative Law and Mediation?
In mediation, there is one "neutral" who helps the disputing parties try to settle their case. The mediator cannot give either party legal advice, and cannot help either side advocate its position. If one side or the other becomes unreasonable or stubborn, lacks negotiating skill, or is emotionally distraught, the mediation can become unbalanced. If the mediator tries to deal with the problem, he is often seen by one side or the other as biased, whether or not that is the case. If the mediator does not find a way to deal with the problem, the mediation can break down or the agreement that results can be unfair. If there are attorneys for the parties at all, they may not be present at the negotiation and their advice may come too late to be helpful.

Collaborative Law on the other hand, was designed to deal more effectively with all these problems, while maintaining the same absolute commitment to settlement as the sole agenda. Each side has quality legal advice and advocacy built in at all times during the process. It is the job of the lawyers to work with their own clients if the clients are being unreasonable to make sure that the process stays positive and productive.

4. What Kind of Information and Documents are Available in the Collaborative Law Negotiations?

Both sides sign a binding agreement to disclose all documents and information that relate to the issues, early and fully and voluntarily. "Hide the ball" and stonewalling are not permitted. All information is shared openly. Attorneys and clients work together to create win–win solutions for all members of the family.

5. Why is Collaborative Law Such an Effective Settlement Process?

The Collaborative Law attorneys have a completely different state of mind about what their job is than traditional lawyers generally bring to their work. We call it a "paradigm shift." Instead of being dedicated to getting the largest possible piece of the pie for their own client, no matter the human or financial cost, collaborative lawyers are dedicated to helping their clients achieve their highest intentions for themselves in their post-divorce restructured families.

Collaborative lawyers do not act as a hired gun. Nor do they take advantage of mistakes inadvertently made by the other side. They expect and encourage the highest good-faith problem-solving behavior from their own clients and themselves.

Collaborative lawyers trust one another. They still owe a primary allegiance and duty to their own clients but they know that the only way they can serve the true best interests of their clients is to behave with, and demand, the highest integrity from themselves, their clients, and the other participants in the process.

Collaborative Law and Collaborative Divorce offer a greater potential for creative problem-solving than does either mediation or litigation, in that only Collaborative Law puts two lawyers in the same room pulling in the same direction to solve the same list of problems. No matter how good a lawyer they are for their client, they cannot succeed as a Collaborative Lawyer unless they also can find solutions to the other party's problems that their client finds satisfactory. This is the special characteristic of Collaborative Law that is found in no other dispute resolution process.

LEGAL SEPARATION

A fourth option for some couples is a legal separation instead of a divorce. Under a legal separation, they divide their property and there may be child support and maintenance, but they are still legally married. A couple may choose this route for several reasons:

1. *Religious reasons.* Some religions frown on divorce. Many people are uncomfortable going against the teachings of their religion.
2. *Health insurance.* Even though COBRA allows the ex-spouse to retain health insurance for three years after the divorce is final, if the ex-spouse is uninsurable, this can be a great concern. A legal separation allows the ex-spouse to remain on the working spouse's health insurance plan.
3. *Not wishing a divorce.* Many couples can't stand living together but they also hate the thought of being divorced. A legal separation allows them to live their separate lives. And some spouses hold the secret thought that the marriage could be put back together. If the marriage turns out to be impossible to salvage, then a divorce can be filed and is easily accomplished as all the details, such as dividing the property, have already been done.

Summary

- Give mediation a chance. Mediation is where you and your spouse meet with a neutral third party to try and reach a settlement. The mediator can be a lawyer, a financial planner or a therapist as long as they have taken at least 40 hours of mediation training.
- If mediation doesn't appeal to you, consider collaborative divorce. It is the latest, most innovative way to settle your divorce. It has been found that collaborative divorce takes less

time and is less costly then traditional approaches. In addition, it helps the family unit retain their dignity and it reduces the trauma and emotional affects on the children.

(Special thanks for contributions to this chapter go to Christine Coates, J.D., nationally known trainer and speaker on mediation from Boulder, CO; Michael Caplan, J.D., a mediator trainer in Boulder, CO; Gary J. Friedman, J.D., of the Center for Mediation and Law, Mill Valley, CA; and Pauline Tesler, J.D., of the American Institute of Collaborative Professionals, Santa Rosa, CA.)

chapter 11

WHAT TO EXPECT: THE PLAYERS AND THE PROCESS

This chapter will serve as a warm-up to the real thing. Each player is identified and each process outlined to help prepare you for what's to come next. Before we delve into the actual procedures, let's first take a look at who the players are:

FINANCIAL DIVORCE SPECIALISTS

The Financial Divorce Specialist can play a valuable role in the mediation process. They can educate the lawyer as to the need for a professional planner. With information from you, the client and the lawyer, the Financial Divorce Specialist

- will examine all assets and liabilities
- may suggest alternative solutions to the attorney and the client.

When appropriate, a Financial Divorce Specialist could attend the mediation session or at least be available by phone and fax.

The Financial Divorce Association in Boulder, Colorado offers training for professionals and certifies them as a Financial Divorce Specialist. The agenda includes an overview of the divorce market, tax laws of divorce, division of property, alimony, child support, pensions, being an expert witness in court, marketing these services, and much more. Also included is hands-on training with the DivorceCalc™ software. Phone: 888-332-3342; or visit their website at: www.FDAdivorce.com.

HIRING AN ATTORNEY

Some couples think they can hire one attorney and save costs. But the fact is if they can't reach a settlement and have to go to court, each spouse will need their own attorney. One-lawyer divorces are ill advised and are prohibited in many states as unethical.

Issues may arise that neither party thought about but that must be resolved. It will be almost impossible for one attorney to help the couple resolve these issues if the solution is advantageous to one party and adverse to the other. In such a case, one of the spouses will have to hire another lawyer.

Most people who go through a divorce have lawyers. But there is a trend in this country that people do not retain lawyers. People who go through divorce without a lawyer are called "pro se." The statistics are that at least 50% of the people who go through divorce or sue each other after the divorce have no lawyer.

PROBLEMS WITH "PRO SE" DIVORCES

Income taxes: Many people do not understand the tax consequences of transferring certain property, such as the house, or stock with a low basis. One of them may be stuck with a huge tax bill.

Missed assets: If the parties don't completely understand the difference between marital and separate property, some property may be transferred without fully understanding the legal options.

Pensions: Sometimes, retirement accounts are the most valuable marital asset. If the parties do not fully understand the retirement plans, they could grossly undervalue what is to be divided. Some also fail to understand the consequences of the death of the employee or the non-employee. In these cases, benefits could revert to the company rather than the beneficiaries the parties intended.

WHAT IS THE FINANCIAL PLANNER'S ROLE?

You will come across many titles for a financial expert: Certified Public Accountant (CPA), financial planner, Certified Financial Planner

(CFP), Chartered Financial Consultant (ChFC), economist, accountant, and Financial Divorce Specialist.

As we mentioned above, the **Financial Divorce Specialist** is a new type of professional. This person is often a Certified Financial Planner who has taken additional intensive training to become skilled in working specifically with people in divorce, becoming part of the divorce team with the attorney, dealing with all the financial issues in each case, and appearing as an expert witness if needed.

The role of a **financial planner,** as opposed to a generic financial expert, is to help people achieve their financial goals regardless of whether they are divorcing, have been divorced, or happily married. After deciding what the goals are, the next step is to look at what needs to be done to achieve those goals. These goals can be from one year to 50 years in the future. Looking that far into the future requires certain assumptions about income, expenses, inflation, interest rates, return on investments, and retirement needs. After the assumptions are made and plugged in, the scenario needs to be reviewed on a regular basis to see if they are still on track.

In other words, the financial planner looks at financial results in the future based on certain assumptions made today. Conversely, the **CPA** typically looks at the details of the scenario as it is today and makes no future projections. These ideologies can certainly be blended for your best interest.

A financial planner is well-versed in interviewing clients to find out what their future goals are, when they want to retire, how much risk they are willing to take with their investments, what kind of a living style they want, what kind of education they want for their children, and so on. **Certified Financial Planners,** on the other hand, are *also* trained in tax issues, estate planning, retirement planning, investment planning, insurance planning, cash flows, and budgeting.

DIVORCE PROCEDURES

The laws governing divorce vary greatly from state to state. While you would want to lean on your attorney for most of the particulars of your state, it is important to have an understanding of the basic process and procedure.

I. Grounds

In every state in this country, divorce is "no fault." That means that either spouse can get a divorce, even if the other spouse doesn't want the divorce. It does not need to be proven that the other spouse was a bad person in order to get a divorce. The language is typically that the marriage is "irretrievably broken" with no chance for reconciliation.

In some states, "fault" could play a role in the division of property, award of custody, award of alimony or child support. It's an intimidating factor in settling a case if one spouse has to testify regarding his or her bad acts.

II. Waiting Periods

A. Residency

In all states, one spouse needs to have been a resident for a certain period of time for the court to have jurisdiction to divorce the couple. The typical length of time is 90 days.

B. "Cooling off" Period

The other time period that states require is the "cooling off period" intended to prevent people from rushing to divorce. In many states the period of time from when you start the case to when you end the case is typically 90 days. Even though that period is relatively short, the average divorce case takes about a year. About 90-95% of divorce cases reach a settlement. If no settlement is reached, the parties go to court and the judge makes the final decision.

III. Temporary Orders

Whether the case takes 90 days or 5 years, the period of time between the beginning and the end of the case is a time when the financial and emotional life of the family goes on. There are children to feed, there are mortgages to pay, and there are insurances to deal with. This is the temporary period. It's during this temporary period that people usually reach settlement about how to manage their lives while they are waiting for the case to be over. If they can't settle, they go to a judge to have a Temporary Orders trial.

A common temporary order is one that orders one spouse to pay support to the other until the divorce trial takes place. Before the judge can grant the motion, it must be shown that support is needed and that the spouse is capable of paying the amount requested.

To show the need and the ability to pay, most states require that a sworn statement (the Financial Affidavit) be prepared, detailing both spouse's living expenses and incomes.

IV. Permanent Orders

Permanent orders are the final divorce orders that dissolve the marriage and enter permanent financial and child based orders. Couples reach the permanent order stage by resolving their situation one of two ways: they either settle or they go to trial.

V. Tax Implications

The tax filing status for each spouse is determined by the legal status (divorced or married) on December 31. If the couple doesn't get divorced until Dec 31, they are divorced for the entire year. If they don't get divorced until Jan 1, they are married for the entire prior year. This creates financial planning opportunities. Taxes can be figured for the couple based on Married, Filing Separately or Head of Household versus a joint return to see which would give the greatest tax benefit.

VI. Approaches to Settlement

A. Parties Direct the Negotiation

Most people who are getting divorced can't talk to each other so this approach doesn't always work. The "pro se" population is generally more able to talk to each other. They are working without lawyers and are trying to settle.

B. Lawyers Direct the Negotiation

One lawyer represents the husband and one represents the wife.

- Settlement letters — the lawyers send letters back and forth.
- Four-way meetings — these are meetings with both lawyers and both spouses to try to reach a settlement.

C. Alternative Dispute Resolution

Alternative dispute resolution is quickly gaining momentum with couples entering divorce. Alternative resolutions include:

- Mediation
- Arbitration
- Collaborative Divorce
- Legal Separation

VII. Trials

If the parties don't settle, then they go to trial and have a judge decide their future. Only about 5% of divorce cases actually go to trial. Whether they settle "on the courthouse steps" or earlier is impossible to ascertain. That fact that about 95% of them settle is good because if they have come to an agreement on their own, they are more likely to honor that agreement than one handed down to them by "the person in the black robe." In one sense, they have taken charge of their own future and it gives them a feeling that they are in control. Going to court takes all control away from them.

All divorce cases are decided by a judge and not a jury (although a couple of states have limited jury trials).

If one or the other of the divorcing couple strongly opposes the judge's decision, they can appeal for either of the following reasons:

- Error of law: A judge's decision can be appealed if one of the parties feels there was an error in the interpretation of the law or if the judge handed down the decision incorrectly.
- Abuse of discretion: A judge's decision can be appealed if one of the parties feels there was an abuse of discretion.

VIII. Discovery

Discovery is the process of gathering information about the nature, scope, and credibility of the opposing party's claim. Discovery procedures include depositions, written interrogatories, and notices to produce various documentation relating to issues which are decided in the case. Many cases are won or lost at the discovery stage.

The theory is that justice is best served if both sides have access to the same facts and evidence. But with a spouse who is knowledgeable about financial affairs and willing and able to manipulate records, discovery can turn into a struggle.

If your spouse works for someone else, be thankful, because tracking down accounts and investments will be easy compared to the situation if the spouse is a self-employed professional or runs his or her own business. Manipulation of financial data may be relatively easy for the self-employed people such as doctors, dentists, lawyers, accountants, financial consultants, stockbrokers, real estate agents, store or factory owners, independent contractors, or someone who runs a cash business.

The law gives your lawyer wide discretion to review tax returns, business and personal records, contracts, canceled checks, credit card receipts, and other documents; and to question your spouse, his or her friends, relatives, and business associates about the spouse's financial dealing.

A. Types of Discovery

There are two types of discovery; informal and formal.

1. Formal Discovery

Formal discovery includes legal procedures such as **depositions, interrogatories** and **requests for production of documents.**

A **deposition** is the sworn testimony of a witness taken outside the court in the presence of lawyers for each side. There is also a court reporter present to record the proceedings and testimony has to be given under oath. Because it is a sworn statement, it becomes part of the record of the case. If you say one thing in the discovery deposition and another thing at the trial, you will have to explain why your answer changed. The parts of the discovery deposition that are in conflict can be read to the witness at trial, and if the change is substantial and unexplained, the overall testimony of the witness is less believable.

Depositions are used for many purposes — for example, to gather information that the witness may have that would be difficult to obtain in a written exchange of questions (interrogatories), to compel a reluctant witness to share information, or to test the competence and reliability of an expert witness, and generally to tie down information given under oath.

Interrogatories are a series of written questions submitted to the other party. Because interrogatories are in writing and do not require the "live" presence of the attorneys and the court reporter, they are used more frequently than depositions. The answers to interrogatories must be under oath and filed within a prescribed period of time.

Interrogatories are commonly used to obtain more information or details about a particular item such as an employment contract or pension plan information.

Requests for production of documents require the spouses and third parties to produce documents necessary to understand the issues in the case.

2. Informal Discovery

Informal discovery can be as simple as one lawyer calling the other lawyer and saying, "Send over to me everything you've got about the Smith case including financial affidavits, tax returns, check stubs, investment statements, list of assets, and anything else we might need to see." And the other lawyer responds, "Okay, you'll have it by Friday."

Well, it might not be quite that simple but if the spouse's lawyer is cooperating, he/she adds to the informal discovery by *voluntarily* providing requested information and documentation. The best lawyers do this without hesitation and give complete relevant financial facts. The lawyer knows he will be required to provide this information anyhow, and he can save time for the client and himself as well as the expense of formal discovery.

The lawyer is within his rights not to disclose information that is not requested, but he cannot go along with intentional deception.

Summary

- Don't hire a lawyer based on his or her low cost or out of friendship. Divorce law is a specialty area of the law and unless your lawyer keeps up with the specific tax laws, the results could be quite costly to you.
- You each need your own lawyer. Ethically, a lawyer should not and cannot represent both of you. Even if you are sure that you'll be able to settle your case and not go to court, what if at the last minute you and your spouse are unable to agree on a specific term? Since your lawyer can only represent one side, but now knows both, you will be faced with having to hire new lawyers and starting the process all over again.
- Consider hiring a Financial Divorce Specialist. A Financial Divorce Specialist is a financial professional who has been trained in the specific financial and tax issues in divorce. They are an integral part of your divorce team and can be a great asset to both you and your attorney.

(Special thanks for contributions to this chapter go to Barbara K. Stark, J.D., a fellow of the American Academy of Matrimonial Lawyers, New Haven, CT.)

the final word

At the start of this book, my objective was to illustrate that divorce could be fair to both parties. As we've discovered, it is also obvious that divorce is rarely easy. Perhaps people should look at what it takes to get divorced before they get married. With all the time, money and emotion involved, it might make potential spouses think harder about whether they are getting married for the right reasons. If they're not, it would allow them to reconsider getting married in the first place.

However, even this knowledge won't stop many from getting married — and then, unfortunately, divorced. There is a type of insanity that seems to surface when a divorce is imminent. Otherwise, why would rational people divorce? Men and women say, and do, things to each other that are horrible — things that they would never have imagined they would say and do to someone they loved and cared for at one time.

Someone once said that the cost of a divorce averages $20,000 per couple. If this is true, Americans are needlessly spending $28 billion dollars on divorce *every year*! And the work force suffers because it's not easy to leave the emotions outside the door of the office. Added to that are the anger, bitterness and vindictiveness that tear families apart.

My vision is that all the professionals work together to minimize the negative impact of divorce. Attorneys help their clients settle out of court. Judges hand down more equitable settlements. Financial advisors provide the essential information to help in the decision-making. And in the end, Americans will have more money available to keep them on the positive side of cash flow instead of being in debt, and children in divorced families will have fewer deep emotional scars. Who knows, maybe the crime rate will even decrease!

Simple? No, but then, when is anything worthwhile simple? What makes common sense? Have patience. Keep learning. I believe in your ability to put it together. Now, it's your turn.

FORMS AND INFORMATION NEEDED TO CONSTRUCT YOUR CASE

Checklist of Information to Gather for Your Attorney:

- ☐ Name, address, and phone number of client
- ☐ Business address and phone number
- ☐ Name, address, and phone number of other party
- ☐ Name and address of lawyer representing other party
- ☐ Dates of birth of each party
- ☐ Date and place of marriage
- ☐ Names and dates of birth of children
- ☐ Prior marriages of each party and details of termination
- ☐ Children of prior marriages and custodial arrangements
- ☐ Length of time lived in this state
- ☐ Existence of prenuptial agreement
- ☐ Grounds for divorce
- ☐ Objectives of each party
- ☐ Date of separation
- ☐ Current employment and place of employment
- ☐ Income of each party
- ☐ Social Security numbers of each party
- ☐ Education/degrees/training of each party
- ☐ Job history and income potential of each party
- ☐ Employee benefits of each party
- ☐ Details of pension and profit-sharing plans for each party

- ☐ Joint assets of the parties, including:
  - Real estate
  - Stocks, bonds, and other securities
  - Bank and savings accounts
  - IRAs
- ☐ Liabilities or debt of each party
- ☐ Life insurance of each party
- ☐ Separate or personal assets of each party
- ☐ Incidences of domestic abuse or threats
- ☐ Financial records which include:
  - Bank statements
  - Tax returns
  - Applications for loans
  - Investment statements
- ☐ Family business records which include:
  - Type of business
  - Shareholders
  - Percent of ownership of business
  - Bank statements of business
  - Tax returns of business
  - Applications for loans
  - Income and balance sheets
  - Financial reports
- ☐ Furniture
- ☐ Patents, royalties, and copyrights
- ☐ Collections, artwork, and antiques
- ☐ Trust funds, annuities, and inheritances
- ☐ Career assets (allowed in some states). Includes education, license or degree, benefit packages, stock options, deferred compensation, vacation, sick leave, bonuses, etc.

FINAL DIVORCE DECREE

After the divorce is final it is too late to find out that additional items should have been negotiated and covered in the final settlement. To make sure that the final divorce decree gives the protection wanted, use this checklist to include those items that pertain to your case.

1. **The Divorce Process**
   - Who pays the legal fees?
   - If the ex-wife must take the ex-husband to court for non-support or for not complying with the divorce decree, will the husband pay the legal fees and court costs? Will there be interest charges?
   - Does the wife want to take back her maiden name?

2. **Property**
   - Who gets which property?
   - Who gets which debt?
   - If the pension is to be divided, has the proper paperwork been prepared?
   - If there is a property settlement note, is it collateralized? Is there interest on it?
   - Does the spouse who gets the house get the whole basis in the house?
   - If the spouse who gets the house needs to sell it immediately, will that person be responsible for the entire capital gains tax?

3. **Maintenance**
   - How much maintenance for how long?
   - If maintenance is not awarded now, can it be awarded later?
   - Will there be life insurance to cover maintenance in the event of the payor's death?

4. **Child Support**
   - How much child support for how long?
   - Will the child support change during college or when visitation times change?
   - Who has custody of the children?
   - What is the visitation schedule?
   - Who pays related expenses for school (transportation, books, etc.) and unusual expenses (lessons, camp, teeth, etc.)?
   - Who will deduct the children on income tax forms?

FORMS

Basic Information

The Basic Information form is for the purpose of data gathering. Many times, some of these pieces of information are missed or overlooked when meeting with your professional for the first time. This form will help you to be more thorough.

BASIC INFORMATION

1. Wife's name _____

Address _____

_____

Age _____

Phone (____)_____ day   (____)_____ evening

Fax (____)_____

E-mail _____

Occupation & no. of years _____

Wife's attorney _____

Phone (____)_____ Fax (____)_____

E-mail _____

2. Husband's name _____

Address _____

_____

Age _____

Phone (____)_____ day   (____)_____ evening

Fax (____)_____

E-mail _____

Occupation & no. of years _____

Husband's attorney _____

Phone (____)_____ Fax (____)_____

E-mail _____

3. Length of marriage (years) _____

4. Number of children _____

    Name   Birthdate

_____

_____

_____

5. Wife's projected gross income _____

    Wife's projected net income _____

6. Husband's projected gross income _____

    Husband's projected net income _____

7. Husband's settlement proposal (attach additional pages as necessary)

    Asset division _____

    Monthly maintenance _____

    How long maintenance will continue _____

    Monthly child support (per child) _____

    How long child support will continue _____

    Contribution to children's college expenses _____

8. Wife's settlement proposal (attach additional pages as necessary)

    Asset division _____

    Monthly maintenance _____

    How long maintenance will continue _____

    Monthly child support (per child) _____

    How long child support will continue _____

    Contribution to children's college expenses _____

9. Residence

Fair market value of home _____

Remaining balance of the mortgage _____

Years remaining to pay _____

Interest rate _____

Monthly payment (PITI) _____

Basis in the house _____

Will the house be sold? _____

If not, who wants to stay in the house? _____

10. Please provide the following information:
List of assets (provide information on each that applies)
- ☐ Checking and Savings accounts
- ☐ CD's
- ☐ Annuities
- ☐ Stocks and Bonds
- ☐ Mutual Funds
- ☐ Real estate (rentals, second home, land, etc.)
- ☐ Limited partnerships
- ☐ Life Insurance policies
- ☐ Family Business
  - Percent of ownership
  - Tax returns
  - Financial statements
- ☐ IRAs
- ☐ 401(k) or other retirement plans
- ☐ Defined benefit pension plan (future payments at retirement)
- ☐ Debt (credit card, loans, etc.)
- ☐ Vehicles
- ☐ Personal possessions
- ☐ Antiques & collectibles
- ☐ Personal or separate property

Last 3 years tax returns
Paycheck stubs
Financial affidavit for husband & wife (shows income & expenses)
Information on pension and retirement plans

ALL INFORMATION IS STRICTLY CONFIDENTIAL

Financial Affidavit

As the backbone of each and every divorce case, the Financial Affidavit helps you to gather all of the pieces of information and financial figures needed in putting your case together.

FINANCIAL AFFIDAVIT

Name _____

1. Job title or occupation _____

2. Primary employer's name _____
   Hours worked per week_____

3. I am paid:

   ☐weekly ☐every other week ☐twice each month ☐monthly

   Amount of each check (gross) _____

4. Monthly gross income _____

5. Monthly payroll deductions

   (Number of exemptions being claimed: _____)

   Federal income tax_____

   Social Security _____

   Medicare_____

   State income tax_____

   Health insurance premium_____

   Life insurance premium _____

   Dental insurance premium_____

   401(k) _____

   Total deductions from this employment_____

6. Net monthly take home pay from primary employer _____

7. Other sources and amounts of income

SOURCE   AMOUNT

_____   _____

_____   _____

8. Deductions from other income sources listed in part 7

DEDUCTIONS   AMOUNT

_____   _____

_____   _____

9. Net monthly income from other sources

10. NET MONTHLY INCOME from ALL sources _____

11. Net monthly income of children _____

12. Income reported on last federal return_____

13. Monthly gross income of other party_____

Monthly net income of other party _____

14. MONTHLY EXPENSES for _____ adult and _____children:

    A. HOUSING

        Rent _____

        First mortgage _____

        Second mortgage_____

        Homeowners fee _____

                TOTAL HOUSING_____

B. UTILITIES

Gas and electric _____

Telephone _____

Water and sewer _____

Trash collection _____

Cable TV _____

TOTAL UTILITIES_____

C. FOOD

Grocery store items _____

Restaurant meals _____

TOTAL FOOD_____

D. MEDICAL (after insurance)

Doctor _____

Dentist _____

Prescriptions _____

Therapy _____

TOTAL MEDICAL_____

E. INSURANCE

Life insurance _____

Health insurance _____

Dental insurance _____

Homeowners _____

TOTAL INSURANCE_____

F. TRANSPORTATION

Vehicle #1 _____

Payment _____

Fuel _____

Repair/maintenance _____

Insurance _____

Parking _____

Vehicle #2 _____

Payment _____

Fuel _____

Repair/maintenance _____

Insurance _____

Parking _____

TOTAL TRANSPORTATION _____

G. CLOTHING _____

TOTAL CLOTHING _____

H. LAUNDRY _____

TOTAL LAUNDRY _____

I. CHILD CARE (and related)

Child care _____

Allowance _____

TOTAL CHILD CARE _____

J. EDUCATION (and related)

For children

School costs _____

Lunches _____

Sports _____

For spouse

Tuition _____

Books and fees _____

TOTAL EDUCATION _____

K. RECREATION

Entertainment _____

Hobbies _____

Vacations _____

Memberships/clubs _____

TOTAL RECREATION _____

L. MISCELLANEOUS

Gifts _____

Hair care/nail care _____

Pet care _____

Books/newspapers _____

Donations _____

TOTAL MISCELLANEOUS _____

M. TOTAL REQUIRED MONTHLY EXPENSES _____

15. DEBTS

	Creditor	Unpaid Balance	Monthly Payment
A.	_____	$ _____	$ _____
B.	_____	$ _____	$ _____
C.	_____	$ _____	$ _____
D.	_____	$ _____	$ _____

16. ASSETS

A. REAL ESTATE

Location_____

Market value _____

Loan_____

Net equity _____

ESTATE

Location_____

Market value _____

Loan_____

Net equity _____

TOTAL REAL ESTATE (NET)_____

B. FURNITURE

Location_____

Market value _____

Location_____

Market value _____

Location_____

Market value _____

TOTAL FURNITURE_____

C. MOTOR VEHICLES

Year/make _____

Market value _____

Loan_____

Net equity _____

Year/make _____

Market value _____

Loan_____

Net equity _____

TOTAL VEHICLES_____

D. BANK ACCOUNTS

Name of bank _____

Current balance_____

Name of bank _____

Current balance_____

Name of bank _____

Current balance_____

Name of bank _____

Current balance_____

TOTAL BANKS_____

E. STOCKS AND BONDS

Stock name _____

No. of shares _____

Market value _____

Stock name _____

No. of shares _____

Market value _____

TOTAL STOCKS/BONDS_____

F. LIFE INSURANCE

Company name_____

Policy number_____

Owner's name _____

Insured's name _____

Beneficiary's name_____

Face value _____

Cash surrender value _____

Company name_____

Policy number_____

Owner's name _____

Insured's name _____

Beneficiary's name_____

Face value _____

Cash surrender value _____

Company name _____

Policy number _____

Owner's name _____

Insured's name _____

Beneficiary's name _____

Face value _____

Cash surrender value _____

TOTAL INSURANCE_____

G. PENSION, PROFIT SHARING, RETIREMENT FUNDS

Plan name _____

Participant name _____

Value _____

Plan name _____

Participant name _____

Value _____

TOTAL PENSION_____

TOTAL ASSETS _____

FINANCIAL AFFIDAVIT CASE STUDY

The following case study will help guide you through the preparation of a Financial Affidavit. As the backbone of each and every divorce case, it becomes part of the recorded documents that are filed with the court.

THE IMPORTANCE OF THE FINANCIAL AFFIDAVIT

Every divorce case starts with the Financial Affidavit. It may be called by different names from state to state but they all include the following:

1. Income from all sources
2. Deductions from income
3. Living expenses
4. Assets
5. Liabilities

Let's look at each of the parts of the Financial Affidavit in the case of Sara and Kevin and how these affect the computer report we produce on the DivorceCalc™ software.

1. INCOME FROM ALL SOURCES

Income includes earned income (W2 income) as well as income from rent, investments, trusts, and business income.

Sara is paid every 2 weeks. Each of her paychecks indicates the following:

Gross earnings		$461.54
Federal taxes	$37.60	
State taxes	$ 9.23	
FICA	$28.62	
Medicare	$ 6.70	
Total deductions		$ 82.15
Net take home pay		$379.39 (every 2 weeks)

Sara earns yearly income of $12,000 per year which, when divided by 26 equals $461.54. But Sara thinks that she should double this number to get her monthly income. So after she doubles each number, her affidavit looks like this:

Gross earnings		$923.08
Federal taxes	$75.20	
State taxes	$18.46	
FICA	$57.24	
Medicare	$13.40	
Total deductions		$164.30
Net take home pay		$758.78

However, Sara has made a very common mistake that often shows up when an individual gets paid every other week or 26 times a year. Since she is paid 26 times per year, her monthly deductions should actually be $178.00 ($164.30 × 13 divided by 12) and her monthly gross is, therefore, $1,000 ($923.08 × 13 divided by 12). After deductions, her monthly net should be $822.00 ($1,000 − $178.00) × 12 or $9,864 per year.

Sara thinks her take home pay is:

$11,077	gross pay
− $1,972	deductions ($164.30 × 12)
$9,105	net take home pay

When it is actually:

$12,000	gross pay
− $2,136	deductions ($178.00 × 12)
$9,864	net take home pay

2. DEDUCTIONS FROM INCOME

Paychecks include mandatory deductions such as: federal tax, state tax, FICA, and Medicare. Some also include deductions for things like a 401(k) contribution, 401(k) loan payback, health insurance, life insurance, union dues, thrift savings account, stock purchase, etc.

The courts allow voluntary contributions to investments like a 401(k), savings plans, and stock purchases to be brought back into cash flow. In other words, we do not have to deduct it from income. This results in higher take-home pay. After all, if Kevin is contributing $917 per month to a 401(k), he still owns that $917 — it is just in a different account. The courts feel that the welfare of the family comes before the building up of Kevin's retirement fund.

On the other hand, a monthly deduction to pay back a loan from a 401(k) is mandatory and must be included as a deduction. Union dues are usually mandatory. And insurance costs should probably be kept as a deduction.

Kevin is paid monthly and earns $110,000 per year or $9,167 per month. His pay stub shows the following deductions:

−	$1,951	Federal income tax
−	$404	State income tax
−	$568	Social Security
−	$133	Medicare
−	$305	Health and dental insurance
−	$375	Stock purchase (ESOP)
−	$450	Savings account
−	$917	401(k)
	$5,103	

$9,167 less deductions of $5,103 leave net take home pay of $4,064 × 12 = $48,768 per year. Now we want to make some corrections.

Kevin is deducting $568 per month for Social Security, which equates to 6.2% of his gross monthly salary. However, that will disappear for the last two months of the year. His average deduction for Social Security should be $454 per month. Kevin's health and dental insurance cost is $305 per month for the family and will continue to keep the children covered on his policy.

Kevin's ESOP is a voluntary investment and the court will allow us to disregard for the purposes of figuring cash flow. His savings account is also voluntary which we can also disregard. Remember, he still has that money — it is just in a different place. His accounts are increasing in value.

Regarding Kevin's 401(k), he is contributing 10% of his salary each month. His company contributes 5% of his salary whether Kevin contributes or not. We can disregard his contribution, which means we have even more take-home pay. But what if Kevin's company only contributes 5% if Kevin contributes at least 5%? It may be important in that case to leave the 401(k) deduction in. For the sake of the following case study, we are going to remove the 401(k) deduction.

A more accurate list of deductions for Kevin is the following:

—	$1,951	Federal income tax
—	$404	State income tax
—	$454	Social Security
—	$133	Medicare
—	$305	Health insurance
	$3,247	

$9,167 less deductions of $3,247 leaves net take home pay of $5,920 × 12 = $71,040 per year.

When we enter the numbers in the DivorceCalc™ software program, we will use $71,040 as Kevin's take-home pay.

3. LIVING EXPENSES

This is the area that generally tends to cause the most concern. Courts talk about "reasonable living expenses." But what is "reasonable?" Reasonable becomes much different to a family who is used to living on $350,000 per year than a family whose total take-home from all sources is less than $60,000 per year. And the situation for the $60,000 per year family is compounded because they now have to set up and pay for two homes instead of one. If there are children still at home, the costs escalate even further as each parent tries to create a home-like atmosphere in both Mom's and Dad's house. This includes duplicate beds, clothes, toys, favorite foods, etc. Maybe even a computer and stereo in each home!

What about the wife who has scrimped on buying clothes for herself for years and now feels that $1,000 per month is a reasonable amount to replenish her wardrobe? Or what about the husband who has worked hard for the family, has never taken much time off, and now wants to play catch up with a scuba-diving trip every chance he gets? And what about the costs for therapy due to the emotional strain of divorce? How long will it last? Can you deduct it from expenses after a year or so?

What about health insurance on the stay-at-home spouse's affidavit? Many times, the health insurance for the family has been an automatic deduction from the working spouse's paycheck. It has never been a bill to be paid each month and many people forget about putting it on the affidavit. *(NOTE: You may have to get a quote for a new policy to enter the correct information.)*

4. ASSETS

Following is a checklist of assets:
- ☐ Checking and savings accounts
- ☐ Certificates of deposit
- ☐ Annuities
- ☐ Stocks and bonds
- ☐ Mutual funds
- ☐ Real estate (rentals, second home, land, etc.)
- ☐ Limited partnerships
- ☐ Life insurance cash value
- ☐ Family business
- ☐ IRAs
- ☐ 401(k) or other retirement plans
- ☐ Defined benefit pension plan (future payments at retirement)
- ☐ Vehicles
- ☐ Personal possessions
- ☐ Antiques & collectibles
- ☐ Personal or separate property
- ☐ Trusts
- ☐ Tax refunds
- ☐ Bonuses yet to be paid
- ☐ Royalties

Most of these are obvious to most people. However, some of them do get left out such as:

- ☐ Life insurance cash value. They may need to find out the most recent accounting from the insurance company.
- ☐ Family business. Most don't have any idea what the family business is worth; they either think it is worth a fortune - or nothing.
- ☐ Defined benefit pension. Many non-working spouses don't understand how pensions work and may not think it is of much value when it may be one of the largest assets they own.
- ☐ Vehicles. If the working spouse has a car furnished by the company and the non-working spouse has a car worth $26,000, how do you handle that? Does the working spouse get $26,000 of another asset as an offset? That doesn't seem quite fair. It may make sense to say that each spouse takes a car, and not put the cars on the list of assets to be divided.
- ☐ Trusts. Be sure to ask about the existence of a trust. Even though it may not be a marital asset, there may be an increase of value to consider.
- ☐ Tax refunds. It is surprising how often tax refunds that come in after the divorce is final are not divided with the other spouse because they were not considered at the time of divorce.
- ☐ Bonuses yet to be paid. If bonuses are a usual occurrence, they may be paid out the following tax year and they might be marital property.
- ☐ Royalties. Are there inventions, printed matter, software, or other items that would create royalties in the future?

5. LIABILITIES

Show all credit card debt, lines of credit, bank loans, loans from parents, etc.

SARA AND KEVIN CASE STUDY

Sara, age 38, and Kevin, age 40, have been married 15 years and they have two sons, ages 11 and 13. Kevin feels that Sara can earn more than she does now. Sara feels it is important to be home when the boys come home from school and that restricts the kind of job she can find.

Let's look at Sara's and Kevin's financial affidavits. Pages 172 to 175 show the abbreviated forms of their financial affidavit for the purposes of this exercise. A complete financial affidavit is shown starting on page 156.

Although more often then not, errors are innocent on the client's part. We will address some of the more common ones as we go through the following case study.

FINANCIAL AFFIDAVIT

Name **SARA**

1. I am paid:

   ☐ weekly ☒ every other week ☐ twice each month ☐ monthly

2. Monthly gross income _____ **$923.08**

3. Monthly payroll deductions

   Federal income tax _____ **75.20** _____

   Social Security _____ **57.23** _____

   Medicare _____ **13.40** _____

   State income tax _____ **18.46** _____

   Total deductions from this employment _____ **$164.29**

4. Net monthly take home pay from primary employer _____ **$758.79**

5. MONTHLY EXPENSES for ___1___ adult and ___2___ children:

   A. HOUSING

   First mortgage _____ **1,487.00** _____ TOTAL **$1,487.00**

   B. UTILITIES _____ **397.00** _____ TOTAL **$397.00**

   C. FOOD

   Grocery store items _____ **600.00** _____

   Restaurant meals _____ **100.00** _____ TOTAL **$700.00**

   D. MEDICAL (after insurance) **90.00** _____ TOTAL **$90.00**

   E. INSURANCE

   Health insurance _____ **250.00** _____ TOTAL **$250.00**

F. TRANSPORTATION

Payment _____ **310.00** _____

Fuel _____ **112.00** _____

Repair/maintenance _____ **50.00** _____

Insurance _____ **80.00** ____TOTAL__ **$552.00**

G. CLOTHING _____ **275.00** ____TOTAL__ **$275.00**

H. EDUCATION for children

School costs _____ **50.00** ____TOTAL__ **$50.00**

I. RECREATION _____ **230.00** ____TOTAL__ **$230.00**

J. MISCELLANEOUS

Gifts _____ **90.00** _____

Hair care/nail care_____ **45.00** _____

Pet care _____ **25.00** _____

Books/newspapers_____ **75.00** _____

Donations_____ **46.00** ____TOTAL__ **$281.00**

K. DEBTS

Creditor	Unpaid Balance	Monthly Payment
Chase Visa	$ **7,853.00**	$ **$300.00**

TOTAL REQUIRED MONTHLY EXPENSES____ **$4,612.00**

× 12 = **$55,344 per year**

FINANCIAL AFFIDAVIT

Name **KEVIN**

1. I am paid:

   ☐ weekly ☐ every other week ☐ twice each month **☒** monthly

2. Monthly gross income _____ **$9,167.00**

3. Monthly payroll deductions

   Federal income tax _____ **1,951.00** _____

   Social Security _____ **446.00** _____

   Medicare_____ **133.00** _____

   State income tax_____ **404.00** _____

   Health insurance_____ **270.00** _____

         Total deductions from this employment _____ **$3,204.00**

4. Net monthly take home pay from primary employer __ **$5,963.00**

5. MONTHLY EXPENSES for ___1___ adult and __2___children:

   A. HOUSING

         Rent _____ **800.00** _____

         Homeownerrs fee _____ **50.00** _____ TOTAL__ **$850.00**

   B. UTILITIES _____ **273.00** _____ TOTAL__ **$273.00**

   C. FOOD

         Grocery store items _____ **150.00** _____

         Restaurant meals _____ **250.00** _____ TOTAL__ **$400.00**

   D. MEDICAL (after insurance) **40.00** _____ TOTAL__ **$40.00**

E. INSURANCE

Life insurance _____ **310.00** _____ TOTAL ___ **$310.00**

F. TRANSPORTATION _____ TOTAL _____

G. CLOTHING _____ **125.00** _____ TOTAL ___ **$125.00**

H. EDUCATION for children

School costs _____ **50.00** _____ TOTAL ___ **$50.00**

I. RECREATION _____ **450.00** _____ TOTAL ___ **$450.00**

J. MISCELLANEOUS

Gifts _____ **60.00** _____

Hair care/nail care _____ **30.00** _____

Books, etc. _____ **60.00** _____

Donations _____ **75.00** _____

Maintenance _____ **2,500.00** _____

Child support _____ **917.00** _____ TOTAL **$3,642.00**

K. DEBTS

Creditor	Unpaid Balance	Monthly Payment
Chase Visa	$ **7,853.00**	$ **$300.00**

TOTAL REQUIRED MONTHLY EXPENSES ___ **$6,440.00**

× 12 = $77,280 per year

COMPARISON OF SARA'S AND KEVIN'S EXPENSES

Kevin is renting an apartment for $800 per month. His utilities (water, sewer, garbage, heat, electricity, cable TV, and telephone) are the same as Sara's.

Kevin's clothing is less than Sara's and this seems to be a typical gender difference. We find that women typically spend more on clothing than men. His hair care is less and he shows nothing for the category of cosmetics.

Kevin's entertainment is higher than Sara's because he is dating again and, has greater expense in that area. Sara's gifts are higher because she has always had the role of buying gifts for others and will probably continue this.

The children live with Sara so she is showing most of the child expenses even though Kevin shows entertainment expenses for the times the children are with him. In comparing the food expense, remember that Sara is feeding three people (including teenagers!), while Kevin's expense is for one. Also notice that Kevin's expense is higher for eating out than Sara's even though hers is for three people. Men typically spend more on eating out.

Kevin shows no expense for car payment, gas and oil, car insurance, or repairs and maintenance because his company furnishes his car and maintains it.

Kevin is including maintenance and child support in his expenses. This does not take into account the tax benefit he receives and does not reflect the accuracy of this expense. Because we enter maintenance and child support in our software as separate expenses so we can show the tax implications, we will subtract those expenses from his financial affidavit.

Without the maintenance and child support expenses, Kevin's expenses are $36,276 that reflects all expenses on his financial disclosure except those deducted from his paycheck. Sara's expenses with the boys are $55,344.

In comparing the difference between Sara's and Kevin's expenses ($55,344 vs. $36,276), we see that Sara's vehicle expenses are $6,624 per year. Kevin doesn't have these expenses as his company pays them. (Should we include this benefit as additional income to him?) Sara will also have to pay for her own health insurance ($3,000 per year). And a conservative estimate for the costs of the two boys is $12,200 per year.

As we saw by reviewing Sara's and Kevin's affidavits, it is important to know exactly how much each is spending and what their spending patterns are. Otherwise, it is impossible to determine what their needs are and how to best meet those needs.

LEGAL DEFINITIONS

Affidavit: A written statement of facts made under oath and signed before a notary public or other officer who has authority to administer oaths.

Alimony: Periodic or lump sum support payments to a former spouse. Also referred to as spousal support. Same as maintenance.

Alternative Dispute Resolution: Ways for parties in a divorce to resolve their disagreements without a trial; usually defined to include negotiation, mediation and arbitration.

Appeal: The process whereby a higher court reviews the proceedings in a lower court and determines whether there was a reversible error. If so, the appellate court amends the judgment or returns the case to the lower court for a new trial.

Appraisal: Procedure for determining the fair market value of an asset when it is to be sold or divided as part of the divorce process.

Arbitration: Submitting a disputed matter for decision to a person who is not a judge. The decision of an arbitrator is usually binding and final.

Assets: Cash, property, investments, goodwill, and other items of value (as defined by state law) that appear on a balance sheet indicating the net worth of an individual or a business.

Basis: Basis is the cost of an asset used to determine tax liabilities. This number is the purchase price, including capital gains and losses, accrued interest, and other fees.

"Best Interests of the Child:" A discretionary legal standard used by judges when making decisions about custody, visitation, and support for a child when the parents are divorcing.

Change of Venue: A change of judges or geographical location, requested by a party to the action who feels that the change is justified by state law.

Child Support: The amount of money paid by a non-custodial parent to the custodial parent for a child's day-to-day expenses and other special needs.

Child Support Guidelines: A series of mathematical formulas that calculate the amount of child support to be paid in some cases. Congress has mandated that states adopt child support guidelines and support enforcement procedures.

Community Property: A form of co-ownership of property by a husband and wife who reside in one of the eight states where community property is recognized. Currently, these eight states follow the community property method: Arizona, California, Idaho, Louisiana, Nevada, New Mexico, Texas, and Washington. The Wisconsin system has similarities.

Complaint: A legal document filed by the plaintiff, stating that the marriage has ended and listing the grounds and claims of the divorce. Also known as a petition.

Contempt of Court: The willful failure to comply with a court order, judgment, or decree by a party to the actions. Contempt of Court may be punishable by fine or imprisonment.

Contested Divorce: Any case where the judge must decide one or more issues that are not agreed to by the parties. All cases are considered contested until all issues have been agreed to.

Court Order: The court's written ruling.

Cross-Examination: The questioning of a witness presented by the opposing party on trial or at a deposition. The purpose is to test the truth of that testimony.

Custody: Usually refers to the parent's right to (1) have a child live with that parent and (2) make decisions concerning the child. Exact meaning varies greatly in different states.

Decree: The final ruling of the judge on an action for divorce, legal separation, or annulment. Same as judgment.

Defendant: The partner in a marriage against whom a divorce complaint is filed. Same as respondent.

Deposition: The testimony of a witness taken out of court under oath and reduced to writing. The most common depositions are discovery depositions taken for the purpose of discovering the facts upon which a party's claim is based or discovering the substance of a witness' testimony prior to trial. The deposition may be used to discredit a witness if he changes his testimony.

Direct Examination: The initial questioning of a witness by the attorney who called him to the stand.

Discovery: Procedures followed by attorneys in order to determine the nature, scope, and credibility of the opposing party's claim. Discovery procedures include depositions, written interrogatories, and notices to produce various documentation relating to issues which are decided in the case.

Dissolution of Marriage: The legal process of ending a marriage. In most states, the legal term for divorce.

Emancipation: The point at which a minor child comes of age. Children are emancipated in most states upon reaching the age of either 18, 19, or 21, or upon marriage, full-time employment, graduation from high school, or entering the armed services. Emancipation is the point where parents have no further legal or financial obligations for a child's support.

Equitable Division of Property: Method of dividing property based on a number of considerations such as length of marriage, differences in age, wealth, earning potential, and health of partners involved that attempts to result in a fair distribution, not necessarily an equal one.

Evidence: Proof presented at a hearing, including testimony, documents, or objects.

Exhibits: Tangible things presented at trial as evidence.

Expert Witness: In court proceedings, professional whose testimony helps a judge reach divorce decisions.

File: To place a document in the official custody of some public official. Also used in the meaning of starting a case.

Foundation: The evidence that must be presented before asking certain questions or offering documentary evidence on trial.

Goodwill: The value of a business beyond its sales revenue, inventory, and other tangible assets; includes prestige, name recognition, and customer loyalty.

Grounds for Divorce: Reasons for seeking a divorce, such as incompatibility, mental cruelty, physical abuse, or adultery. While some states allow fault grounds for divorce, all states have some form of no-fault divorce.

Guardian-ad-Litem: An individual, usually an attorney, appointed by the court to advocate the rights and interests of the children in a divorce — most often when the parents are unable to arrange a custody agreement.

Hearing: Any proceeding before a judicial officer.

Illiquid Asset: Describes an asset that cannot easily be converted into cash; the opposite of liquid. Illiquid assets can be converted into cash, but usually only after a period of time and often at a loss in value.

Interrogatories: A series of written questions served upon the opposing party in order to discover certain facts regarding the disputed issues in a matrimonial proceeding.

Joint Custody: Any arrangement which gives both parents legal responsibility for the care of a child. In some states, it also means shared rights to the child's companionship.

Joint Property: Property held in the name of more than one person.

Judgment: The order of the court on a disputed issue; same as decree.

Jurisdiction: The power of the court to rule upon issues relating to the parties, their children or their property.

Legal Separation: Court ruling on division of property, spousal support, and responsibility to children when a couple wishes to separate but not to divorce. A legal separation is most often desired for religious or medical reasons. A decree of legal separation does not dissolve the marriage and does not allow the parties to remarry.

Maintenance: Spousal support; same as alimony.

Marital Agreement: A contract signed by a couple usually before marriage that lists the assets and liabilities each partner is bringing into the marriage and provides a framework for financial limits to rights of support, property, and inheritance after the marriage and in the event of a divorce or death. Also called prenuptial or antenuptial agreement.

Marital Property: Accumulated income and property acquired by the spouses during the marriage, subject to equitable division by the court. States will vary on their precise definition of what is to be included in marital property, sometimes excepting property acquired by gift or inheritance. (See *community property* and *equitable division of property*.)

Mediation: A non-adversarial process in which a husband and wife are assisted in reaching their own terms of divorce by a neutral third party trained in divorce matters. The mediator has no power to make or enforce decisions.

Modification: A change in the judgment, based on a change of circumstances.

Motion: An application to the court for an order. May be written or oral.

No-Fault Divorce: A marriage dissolution system whereby divorce is granted without the necessity of proving one of the parties guilty of marital misconduct.

Order: A ruling by the court.

Petition: A written application for particular relief from the court. In some jurisdictions complaint for divorce is entitled "petition for dissolution."

Petitioner (Plaintiff): The party who filed the Petition (Complaint).

Plaintiff: The spouse who initiates the legal divorce process by filing a complaint stating that the marriage is over and listing the grounds and claims against the other spouse. Same as petitioner.

Privilege: The right of a spouse to make admissions to an attorney, clergyman, psychiatrist, or others as designated by state law that are not later admissible in evidence.

Property Settlement Note: A note from the payer to the payee for an agreed-upon length of time with reasonable interest. It is still considered division of property, so the payor does not deduct it from taxable income. The payee does not pay taxes on the principle, only on the interest. It is important to collateralize this note.

Pro Se: A party who is representing him or herself in a lawsuit.

Pro Se Divorce: A divorce wherein the divorcing partners represent themselves in court (with or without a mutually agreeable separation agreement) without the assistance of attorneys.

Qualified Domestic Relations Order (QDRO): A court ruling earmarking a portion of a person's retirement or pension fund payments to be paid to his/her ex-spouse as part of a division of marital assets. Payments are made directly to the non-employee ex-spouse by the fund administrator at the time of divorce or at the time the employee's retirement payments are to begin.

Rebuttal: The introduction of evidence at a trial that is in response to new matter raised by the defendant at an earlier stage of the trial.

Respondent (Defendant): The party defending against a divorce Petition (Complaint).

Retainer: Money paid by the client to the lawyer or expert witness to obtain a commitment from the lawyer or expert witness to handle the client's case. A retainer can be a deposit against which the lawyer or expert witness charges fees as they are earned.

Rules of Evidence: The rules that govern the method of presentation and admissibility or oral and documentary evidence at court hearings or depositions.

Separate Property: Generally considered any property owned before marriage (earned or acquired by gift or inheritance), acquired during marriage by one partner using only that partner's separate property, or earned after a formalized separation. This definition will vary from state to state.

Separation Agreement: The legal document listing provisions for peace between the divorcing couple, division of property, spousal support, and responsibility for children of the marriage. The couple's agreement or court-ordered terms are part of the divorce decree.

Settlement Agreement: Same as separation agreement.

Spousal Support: Money paid by one partner to the other for the recipient's support following a divorce. Support may be mandated for a specific period of time (long-term or short-term) and is based on the needs of the recipient, ability to pay, and economic differences between the partners. Also called alimony or maintenance.

Stipulation: An agreement between the parties or their counsel, usually relating to matters of procedure.

Subpoena: A court order requiring a person's appearance in court or deposition as a witness or to present documents or other evidence for a case.

Temporary Orders: Orders granting relief between the filing of the lawsuit and the judgment. Automatic in some states. Also called Pendente Lite Orders.

Testimony: Statements under oath by a witness in a court hearing or deposition.

Traditional Marriage: A marriage in which the wife has either never worked or earns much less than her husband.

Trial: The time when a judge hears the contested permanent or temporary issues, with supporting evidence and witnesses, in a couple's divorce decisions. The judge may take a few hours or a few weeks to review the information presented, and issue a court opinion.

Alabama

Alabama State Bar
415 Dexter Avenue
PO Box 671
Montgomery, AL 36101
334-269-1515

Alaska

Alaska Bar Association
PO Box 100279
Anchorage, AK 99510
907-272-7469

Arizona

American Arbitration Association
Phoenix Regional Office
320 North Central Avenue, Suite 2100
Phoenix, AZ 85012
602-734-9333

State Bar of Arizona
111 W. Monroe, Suite 1800
Phoenix, AZ 85003
602-252-4804

Arkansas

Arkansas Bar Association
400 W. Markham
Little Rock, AR 72201
501-375-4606

California

American Arbitration Association
Los Angeles Regional Office
725 South Figueroa Street, Suite 2400
Los Angeles, CA 90017
213-362-1900

American Arbitration Association
Orange County, CA Regional Office
2030 Main Street
Irvine, CA 92714
949-251-9836

American Arbitration Association
San Diego Regional Office
600 B Street, Suite 1450
San Diego, CA 92101
619-239-3051

American Arbitration Association
San Francisco Regional Office
One Sansome Street, 16th Floor
San Francisco, CA 94104
415-981-3901

State Bar of California
180 Howard Street
San Francisco, CA 94105-1639
415-538-2000

Colorado

American Arbitration Association
Denver Regional Office
1675 Broadway, Suite 2550
Denver, CO 80202
303-831-0823

Colorado Bar Association
1900 Grant Street, Suite 900
Denver, CO 80203
303-860-1115

Connecticut
American Arbitration Association
Hartford Regional Office
111 Founders Place, 17th Floor
East Hartford, CT 06108
860-289-3993

Connecticut Bar Association
30 Bank Street
PO Box 350
New Britain, CT 06050
860-223-4400

Delaware
Delaware State Bar Association
301 North Market Street
Wilmington, DE 19801
302-658-5279

District of Columbia
American Arbitration Association
Washington, DC Regional Office
601 Pennsylvania Avenue NW,
Suite 700
Washington, DC 20004
202-737-9191

Bar Association of the District of Columbia
1225 19th Street NW, Suite 800
Washington, DC 20036
202-223-6600

District of Columbia Bar
1250 H Street NW, 6th Floor
Washington, DC 20005
202-737-4700

Florida
Florida Bar
651 E. Jefferson Street
Tallahassee, FL 32399
850-561-5600

American Arbitration Association
Miami Regional Office
799 Brickell Plaza, Suite 600
Miami, FL 33131
305-358-7777

American Arbitration Association
Orlando Regional Office
315 East Robinson Street, Suite 290
Orlando, FL 32801
407-648-1185

Georgia
American Arbitration Association
Atlanta Regional Office
2200 Century Parkway, Suite 300
Atlanta, GA 30345
404-325-0101

State Bar of Georgia
104 Marietta Street NW, Suite 100
Atlanta, GA 30303
404-527-8700

Hawaii
American Arbitration Association
Honolulu Regional Office
810 Richards Street, Suite 641
Honolulu, HI 96813
808-531-0541

Hawaii State Bar Association
1132 Bishop Street, Suite 906
Honolulu, HI 96813
808-537-1868

Idaho
Idaho State Bar
PO Box 895
Boise, ID 83701
208-334-4500

Illinois

American Arbitration Association
Chicago Regional Office
225 N. Michigan Avenue, Suite 1840
Chicago, IL 60601
312-616-6560

Illinois State Bar Association
424 S. 2nd Street
Springfield, IL 62701
217-525-1760

Indiana

Indiana State Bar Association
One Indiana Square, Suite 530
Indianapolis, IN 46204
317-639-5465

Iowa

Iowa State Bar Association
521 E. Locust
Des Moines, IA 50309
515-243-3179

Kansas

Kansas Bar Association
1200 SW Harrison Street
Topeka, KS 66612
785-234-5696

Kentucky

Kentucky Bar Association
514 W. Main Street
Frankfort, KY 40601
502-564-3795

Louisiana

American Arbitration Association
New Orleans Regional Office
1100 Poydras Street
New Orleans, LA 70163
504-522-8781

Louisiana State Bar Association
601 St. Charles Avenue
New Orleans, LA 70130
504-566-1600

Maine

Maine State Bar Association
124 State Street
Augusta, ME 04330
207-622-7523

Maryland

Maryland State Bar Association
520 W. Fayette Street
Baltimore, MD 21201
410-685-7878

Massachusetts

American Arbitration Association
Boston Regional Office
133 Federal Street, Floor 11
Boston, MA 02110
617-451-6600

Massachusetts Bar Association
20 West Street
Boston, MA 02111
617-338-0500

Michigan

American Arbitration Association
Southfield, MI Regional Office
27777 Franklin Road, Suite 1150,
11th Floor
Southfield, MI 48034
248-352-5500

State Bar of Michigan
306 Townsend Street
Lansing, MI 48933
517-346-6300

Minnesota

American Arbitration Association
Minneapolis Regional Office
200 South 6th Street,
700 Pillsbury Center
Minneapolis, MN 55402
612-332-6545

Minnesota State Bar Association
600 Nicollet Mall #380
Minneapolis, MN 55402
612-333-1183

Mississippi

Mississippi State Bar
643 N. State Street
Jackson, MS 39202
601-948-4471

Missouri

American Arbitration Association
Kansas City Regional Office
120 West 12th Street, Suite 410
Kansas City, MO 64105
816-221-6401

American Arbitration Association
St. Louis Regional Office
100 N. Broadway, Suite 1820
St. Louis, MO 63102
314-621-7175

Missouri Bar
PO Box 119
Jefferson City, MO 65102
573-635-4128

Montana

State Bar of Montana
PO Box 577
Helena, MT 59624
406-442-7660

Nebraska

Nebraska State Bar Association
635 S. 14th Street, PO Box 81809
Lincoln, NE 68501
402-475-7091

Nevada

State Bar of Nevada
600 E. Charleston Blvd
Las Vegas, NV 89104
702-382-2200

New Hampshire

New Hampshire Bar Association
112 Pleasant Street
Concord, NH 03301
603-224-6942

New Jersey

American Arbitration Association
Somerset Regional Office
220 Davidson Avenue, 1st Floor
Somerset, NJ 08873
732-215-732

New Jersey State Bar Association
New Jersey Law Center
1 Constitution Square
New Brunswick, NJ 08901
732-249-5000

New Mexico

State Bar of New Mexico
5121 Masthead NE
Albuquerque, NM 87109
505-797-6000

New York

New York State Bar Association
1 Elk Street
Albany, NY 12207
518-463-3200

American Arbitration Association
Garden City, NY Regional Office
666 Old Country Road
Garden City, NY 11530
516-222-1660

American Arbitration Association
New York Regional Office
335 Madison Avenue, Floor 10
New York, NY 10017
212-716-5800

American Arbitration Association
Syracuse Regional Office
231 Saline Meadows Parkway, Suite 135
North Syracuse, NY 13212
315-457-4249

American Arbitration Association
White Plains, NY Regional Office
399 Knollwood Road
White Plains, NY 10603
914-946-1119

North Carolina
American Arbitration Association
Charlotte Regional Office
200 South College Street, Suite 1800
Charlotte, NC 28202
704-347-0200

North Carolina Bar Association
8000 Weston Parkway
Cary, NC 27513
919-677-0561

North Carolina State Bar
208 Fayetteville Street Mall
PO Box 25908
Raleigh, NC 27611
919-828-4620

North Dakota
State Bar Association of North Dakota
504 N. Washington Street
Bismarck, ND 58501
701-255-1404

Ohio
American Arbitration Association
Cincinnati Regional Office
250 E. 5th Street, Suite 420
Cincinnati, OH 45202
513-241-8434

American Arbitration Association
25050 Country Club Blvd
North Olmstead, OH 44070
440-716-2220

Ohio State Bar Association
1700 Lake Shore Drive
Columbus, OH 43204
800-282-6556

Oklahoma
Oklahoma Bar Association
1901 N. Lincoln Blvd.
PO Box 53030
Oklahoma City, OK 73152
405-416-7000

Oregon
Oregon State Bar
5200 SW Meadows Road
Lake Oswego, OR 97035
503-620-0222

Pennsylvania
American Arbitration Association
Philadelphia Regional Office
230 S. Broad Street, 12th Floor
Philadelphia, PA 19102
215-732-5260

American Arbitration Association
Pittsburgh Regional Office
2 Gateway Center
603 Stanwix Street, Suite 1382
Pittsburgh, PA 15222
412-261-3617

Pennsylvania Bar Association
100 South Street, Box 186
Harrisburg, PA 17108
717-238-6715

Rhode Island
American Arbitration Association
Providence Regional Office
950 Warren Avenue
East Providence, RI 02914
401-435-7474

Rhode Island Bar Association
115 Cedar Street
Providence, RI 02903
401-421-5740

South Carolina
South Carolina Bar
950 Taylor Street
Columbia, SC 29202
803-799-6653

South Dakota
State Bar of South Dakota
222 E. Capitol Avenue
Pierre, SD 57501
605-224-7554

Tennessee
American Arbitration Association
Nashville Regional Office
211 7th Avenue N.
Nashville, TN 37203
615-256-5857

Tennessee Bar Association
221 4th Avenue N, Suite 400
Nashville, TN 37219
615-383-7421

Texas
American Arbitration Association
Dallas Regional Office
13455 Noel Road
Dallas, TX 75240
972-774-6947

American Arbitration Association
Houston Regional Office
1331 Lamar, Suite 1180
Houston, TX 77010
713-739-1302

State Bar of Texas
1414 Colorado Street
Austin, TX 78701
512-463-1463

Utah
American Arbitration Association
Salt Lake City Regional Office
645 S. 200 E.
Salt Lake City, UT 84111
801-531-9748

Utah State Bar
645 S. 200 E., Suite 310
Salt Lake City, UT 84111
801-531-9077

Vermont
Vermont Bar Association
35-37 Court Street
Box 100
Montpelier, VT 05601
802-223-2020

Virginia

Virginia Bar Association
701 E. Franklin Street, Suite 1120
Richmond, VA 23219
804-644-0041

Virginia State Bar
707 E. Main Street, Suite 1500
Richmond, VA 23219
804-775-0500

Washington

American Arbitration Association
Seattle Regional Office
701 Pike Street, Suite 950
Seattle, WA 98101
206-622-6435

Washington State Bar Association
2101 4th Avenue, Suite 400
Seattle, WA 98121
206-443-9722

West Virginia

West Virginia Bar Association
PO Box 2162
Huntington, WV 25722
304-522-2652

West Virginia State Bar
2006 Kanawha Blvd., E.
Charleston, WV 25311
304-558-2456

Wisconsin

State Bar of Wisconsin
5302 Eastpark Blvd.
Madison, WI 53718
608-257-3838

Wyoming

Wyoming State Bar
500 Randall Avenue
PO Box 109
Cheyenne, WY 82003
307-632-9061

recommended reading

Available at: www.superbookdeals.com

Robert E. Alberti & Bruce Fisher: *Rebuilding: When Your Relationship Ends, 3rd Edition*
  1-88623-017-X

Diana Mercer: *Your Divorce Advisor: A Lawyer and a Psychologist Guide You through the Legal and Emotional Landscape of Divorce*
  0-68487-068-1

M. Gary Neuman & Patricia Romanowski: *Helping Your Kids Cope with Divorce the Sandcastles Way*
  0-67977-801-2

Mira Kirshenbaum: *Too Good to Leave, Too Bad to Stay: A Step-By-Step Guide to Helping You Decide whether to Stay in or Get out of Your Relationship, Reprint Edition*
  0-45227-535-0

Lee Raffel: *Should I Stay or Go?*
  0-80922-513-1

Carol Ann Wilson & Edwin Schilling III: *The Survival Manual for Women in Divorce: 185 Questions and Answers about Your Rights and: Common Property, Child Custody, Alimony & Debt, Child Support, Retirement Benefits, and Much More!*
  0-96267-906-2

Carol Ann Wilson & Edwin Schilling III: *The Survival Manual for Men in Divorce: 185 Questions and Answers about Your Rights and: Common Property, Child Custody, Alimony & Debt, Child Support, Retirement Benefits, and Much More!*
  0-96267-907-0

Carol Ann Wilson & Ginita Wall: *ABCs of Divorce for Women*
  0-96267-905-4

Carol Ann Wilson, CFP®, is a recognized specialist in marital financial issues and a pioneer in the field of divorce financial planning. Her pre-divorce consulting company has been in business since 1985. She has served as an expert witness in court in over 120 divorce cases nationwide.

In 1993, she founded the Institute for Certified Divorce Planners to train lawyers, accountants, and financial professionals in the financial issues of divorce. She is now the President of the Financial Divorce Association, Inc.

As an advocate of Collaborative Divorce, she is active in the International Association of Collaborative Professionals.

Carol Ann frequently serves as a speaker and faculty member of high-ranked legal and financial organizations and has been published in many professional journals.

She is the co-author of *ABCs of Divorce for Women, Survival Manual for Men in Divorce, Survival Manual for Women in Divorce, 40 Tips for Surviving Your Divorce,* and *Dollars and Sense of Divorce.* She is also the author of *The Financial Guide to Divorce Settlement.*

Carol Ann has appeared on the Regis Philbin Show, Geraldo, Lifetime Live, CNBC Financial News, and numerous radio programs.

For more information:

Carol Ann Wilson, CFP®
Financial Divorce Association, Inc.
906 Cranberry Ct
Longmont, CO 80503
303-774-1225 or 888-332-3342
www.FDAdivorce.com